The Orvis Wing-Shooting Handbook

The Orvis Wing-Shooting Handbook

Bruce Bowlen

The Lyons Press

Printed in the United States of America

20 19 18 17 16 15 14 13 12

ISBN: 0–941130–05–3

Library of Congress Cataloging-in-Publication Data

Bowlen, Bruce
    The Orvis wing-shooting handbook.
    Includes index.
    1. Shooting. 2. Shotguns. I. Title.
SK37.B68 1985   799.2'4   85-17084

Contents

Introduction

For the past twelve years I have helped students at the Orvis Upland Shooting School improve their shotgunning skills. My experience has convinced me of one thing: most field gunners do not have a sense of what they are doing right or wrong, why they hit one bird and miss the next. The answer to their problem lies in the fact that they have no clearly defined technique.

All too often, my students adopt a fatalistic attitude about their shooting. "He's a natural shot," or "I can't hit my hat today." They resign themselves to the whims of fate that seem to govern their shooting. One day they can't miss and the next day they can't hit the proverbial barn door.

But shooting is *not* governed by the fates. We can learn to improve our shooting skills and tailor our equipment to improve our odds. The all-too-prevalent attitude in this country is that good shots are born. The English have quite a different view. They believe that wing shooting is a skill that can be taught; that there is a right and a wrong way to swing a shotgun, just as there is a right and a wrong way to swing a golf club. Granting latitude for stylistic quirks, they believe there is a method to field shooting. I have to side with the British. Good wing shots are not always born. You can learn to be a good shot. Certainly some lucky folks have better eye–hand coordination and timing than the rest of us, but we can all learn to improve our technique and hone our native skills. What is important is that we understand the basics of good wing shooting and know how to practice productively.

The basic theory and style of shooting that will be outlined herein has been taken primarily from the British. More specifically, I have borrowed from *Churchill's Game Shooting*, by Macdonald Hastings, the

Holland and Holland film "Good Shooting," and personal instruction from Rex Gage, former Director of the Holland and Holland Shooting School, and Michael Rose, Senior Instructor at the West London Shooting School. I make no pretext about having authored the theory or style. During twelve years of teaching one certainly develops his own means of conveying the message, and I believe I've made certain modifications to the English doctrine, but the theory is not new and certainly not original with me.

I do not want to sound like an expatriate. I am not saying that Americans are lousy wing shots, only that the English take a different attitude toward shooting. They treat it like any other eye–hand activity, like golf or tennis. Most Americans think nothing of going to a golf pro to help them with their slice or hook, but we are embarrassed about the need to go to a pro to help us with our shotgun swing.

I do not consider myself to be a shooter of any special ability. My own natural gifts of coordination and timing are very average. Somewhere along the way I have made all the mistakes a shooter could make. Only through diligence and practice have I been able to develop into a passable field shot. I make this statement not out of modesty but to give the reader an insight into my development as a wing shooter and an instructor. I believe not being a natural shot has made me a better teacher. It is my belief that in many instances the gifted, natural athlete is not the best teacher. It can be difficult for the natural to identify and sympathize with a student's mistakes. What has prompted me to write this book are my insights into the problems encountered by average field gunners.

This book is intended as a concise guide for the field gunner. The emphasis will be on shooting, not hunting. In no respect is this an exhaustive treatise on the subject of wing shooting. I hope to be able to offer some guidance to the field gunner in choosing his equipment and developing a shooting technique that will be practical and efficient.

1

A Shotgun Didn't Win the West

We are a nation of rifle shooters. The "blam, blam, blam" that rang through the theater during Saturday-afternoon matinees was not the sound of a twelve bore, but the report of a Winchester or a Colt. Oh, occasionally some oaf would carry a scatter gun, but it was never our hero. The character who resorted to a shotgun was invariably the protagonist's sidekick, a poor boob who lacked the nerves of steel and eagle eye necessary to perform the shooting wizardry that kept us transfixed in our seats. Is it any wonder we prefer the rifleman image?

What was the first gun you fired? Very likely a .22 rifle. What were you taught? Hopefully, you were given basic safety instruction, but in terms of shooting technique, what were you coached to do? Put the front sight in the center of the peep or buckhorn rear sight and align the sights with the bull's eye on your target, or the red and white label on the soup can. Once the sight picture was correct, hold everything steady and squeeze the trigger ever so carefully. Don't wiggle, hold it steady, exhale slowly and keep those sights on the mark. Well, something like that anyway; hopefully, your mentor was more knowledgeable of rifle technique than I. If you missed your target you tried again and were careful to hold everything steadier and more carefully align your sights. Through practice and your coach's encouragement you eventually learned to hold your rifle steady and aim with real precision.

This early training leaves an indelible mark on most of us. We are under its influence all our shooting lives, whether we are conscious of its influence or not. There is a strong inclination to apply this early training to all subsequent shooting situations.

There's an enormous difference between shooting a single projectile through a rifled barrel and shooting a charge of shot through a smooth

1

bore. The gulf seems very apparant intellectually. We can enumerate the differences between rifle and shotgun technique with ease. When we are actually pulling the trigger, however, the distinction seems to get fuzzy. Most people seem to find it difficult to forget that early rifle training. All well and good if we have a rifle in our hands, but not so good if we have a shotgun.

We must segregate our wing-shooting techniques from rifle and pistol techniques first and foremost. Within the framework of shotgunning we must also be careful to keep things segregated. The tools and techniques appropriate to the trap field may not work so well on the skeet field or in the dove field. Obvious, you say; I couldn't agree more, extremely obvious. Why is it then that we find shooters trying to use their trap or skeet techniques, or equipment, in the game field? The style of shooting and equipment should be tailored to the shooting environment. This book is written for the field shotgunner. I make no claim about the applicability of the technique or tools to any other shooting situation.

My point is a simple one. Rifle, trap, skeet and wing shooting in the field are distinctly different and require different techniques. I am waving the banner of the field gunner because it is my impression that most of what has been written in this country about shotgunning has not drawn this distinction clearly enough. You may be an Olympic Gold Medal winner in cross-country skiing, but if you take your skinny little skis and your cross-country kick and glide technique and try to apply it to ski jumping or downhill, you could kill yourself. Yet all three are surely skiing. The distinction that has been left particularly fuzzy is that between the game field and the competitive clay target arena. I am told that skeet sharpens the skills of the upland gunner, and trap is great practice for waterfowl enthusiasts. I will try to enumerate what I feel are the basic differences between field and competitive shooting in the next chapter.

2

Field Shooting Versus Skeet And Trap

Although skeet and trap began as practice mediums for field gunning, they have evolved into ends in themselves. Because of the popularity of these clay target games, many people are introduced to a shotgun on the trap or skeet field. These shooting games differ from game shooting in one principal regard: predictability. The field gunner seldom knows when a grouse will flush or a duck will swing in over his decoys. He does not know how fast the bird will be flying, its range, its angle of flight, or when any, or all, of these things may change. A skeet shooter knows when the target will fly. Its speed, range, and angle of flight are all known in advance. A trap shooter knows everything except the exact angle of flight. Skeet and trap are so predictable that most shooters in this country choose to pre-shoulder the gun. They determine when the target will be launched so they get the gun to shoulder and cheek before calling for the target. This eliminates the necessity for a gun mount coincident with the flight of the bird. Yet good gun-mounting technique is at the very core of the field gunner's system.

In no regard am I trying to detract from the abilities or techniques of skeet or trap shooters. I have the greatest admiration for their abilities. Skeet and trap are both wonderful shooting games. My only point is that they are formalized shooting situations with specific rules. The techniques that have evolved around skeet and trap are specifically suited to the rules of those games. A field shooter needs a technique that is specifically tailored to his game.

Above all else, the field gunner needs a system that is simple, one that will allow him to successfully coordinate many variables in a split-second. He needs a technique that will utilize to full advantage the marvelous capabilities of his eye and hand and requires a minimum of thought. An accomplished field shooter relies on natural eye–hand coordination and a gun-mounting technique, or swing, that has been practiced to develop muscle memory. There is no cognitive element in the system. His technique must be designed as much for flexibility as for precision. The field shooter must be able to cope with an infinite range of targets. The competitive clay-target shooter has a different problem. There are fewer variables, but to be competitive, he needs a system that will be extremely consistent within the parameters of the game. The competitive shooter does not need flexibility so much as he needs precision.

The English style of shooting is well suited to the field. It is simple and it is versatile. It relies on natural eye–hand coordination. At the heart of the system is one well founded assumption, that we all have the ability to point. Anyone can look at an object and, with surprising accuracy, point right at it. We do not have to sight down a finger and look at the relationship of the finger to the object and make corrections. We are not visually conscious of the finger as we point. We keep our eyes fixed on the object we wish to bring attention to and the finger is brought into proper alignment without any real conscious effort. This is an example of natural eye–hand coordination.

It is eye–hand coordination that allows us to hit a golf ball, or a tennis ball, or a baseball. We rely on it constantly, yet in most instances we are unaware of it. It is one of the marvelous gifts that we take for granted. Everyone has eye–hand coordination. Those lucky few who have a high degree of eye–hand coordination are the so-and-so's that find wing shooting easy. Don't be discouraged if you are of average ability. Everyone can improve their eye–hand skills with practice. Eye–hand coordination is an important element in every type of shooting.

The English system is unique because of its reliance on this natural pointing instinct. The English technique is the only one that unequivocally instructs the shooter *not to look at the gun*. Most American shooters want to blend the natural eye–hand capabilities with an aiming technique. It is my belief that the pure eye–hand technique is superior in the field because of its simplicity and flexibility.

Unfortunately, most American shooters seem, consciously or unconsciously, to think of shooting and aiming as being synonymous. By aim, I mean an attempt to account visually for both target and gun at the instant of fire. This is a product of early rifle training. This propensity to aim is at the root of many field shooters' problems. The problem with aiming in most field situations is that a flight plan is not filed in advance. Aiming diverts the shooter's eye from the bird and tends to slow his response to the trigger. Aiming is too complex a system for most field-shooting situations. *The single most important rule in field shooting is to keep your eye on the bird and not on the barrel.*

The eye is not capable of keeping the bird and the barrel both in sharp focus. When the eye is focused on a target at typical shotgun range, twenty-five to thirty yards, the bead on the barrel, twenty-five to thirty inches away, is a hazy blur. If we aim, visual attention will shift to the barrel and the eye will try to clarify the fuzzy image of the bead. As this is accomplished, the target becomes the blurred image, and we momentarily lose close track of its position. Like a camera lens, the eye's depth of field is limited. We do not have sufficient depth of field to accomodate both barrel and bird. The eye is similar to a camera lens in another regard: changes in focus are not made instantaneously. Just as it takes a moment to rotate the barrel of a camera lens to change the focus, the eye requires a brief moment to shift its focus. What usually happens when a shooter *aims* (rather than *points*) at a moving target is that his attention shifts from target to barrel just as he is ready to pull the trigger. And, when the shooter tries to clear up the fuzzy image of his gun in an attempt to aim, he will generally slow, or stop, his swing. It is this attempt to be too precise that gets many field shooters into trouble.

Try pointing at a blackbird, or pigeon, as it flies overhead. As you make the point you won't be visually conscious of your hand. Now double check yourself by looking down at your finger and back to the bird. When you look back to the bird you'll find your finger has fallen behind. It's the same with a shotgun. The problem with this visual confirmation, or aim, in field shooting is that it distracts your eye from a moving object that has no set pattern. As we look down to the gun and try to clarify the fuzzy image of the barrel we lose track of the bird and usually slow or stop our swing.

The field gunner must develop confidence in his instinctive ability to point, to trust his natural eye–hand coordination. Does a golfer look at the club head as he hits the ball? Does a tennis player look back at his racket when returning a serve? The key to good field shooting is learning to keep your eye on the bird.

The blend of pointing and aiming that prevails in this country seems more amenable to the competitive forms of clay-target shooting, where some of the variables have been eliminated. Each station on a skeet field, for example, presents the shooter with a known shooting problem. The shooter can learn to move his gun at a speed and in a direction that is proper for that particular problem. With practice the shooter requires less and less visual assistance to make his alignment. I have been told that the world-renowned skeet shooter, Fred Missildine, could consistently break targets on the skeet field while blindfolded. The skeet shooter practices a series of shots and, if he gets good enough, he may be able to do it with his eyes closed. To be able to aim effectively you must know where the target is, or will be, at the instant of fire. To aim you must sacrifice some of your concentration on the target in order to account visually for the gun. The skeet shooter can afford to be distracted by the gun because of the repetitive nature of his game. Through practice he has learned where the target will be at all times and has developed the muscle memory necessary to move in cadence with the target whether his eye is on the clay or not. The skeet shooter can practice all the shots he will ever see on the skeet field frequently enough to allow him to develop a specific muscle pattern for each one.

Skeet shooting is not easy, but it is predictable. The skeet shooter practices sixteen specific shots, learning to execute each with a consistency that can only be dreamed of by the field gunner. Many shots presented in the field are easy by skeet standards, but the field gunner never knows what the shot will be. The bird may flare, changing angle and speed simultaneously. The field gunner is not dealing with a target that flies in straight lines. He cannot practice specific shots. He must practice a technique that will successfully accommodate the infinite variety of shots that await him.

3

Basic Technique

Every shooter is looking for the one trick that will keep him from ever missing again. The more naïve the shooter, the more likely he is to be looking for the little bit of magic that will make him a great shot. Why is it that perfectly intelligent people have such totally unrealistic expectations when it comes to shooting? There are no magic formulas. To be a successful shooter, you must understand the basic technique involved and practice enough to maintain muscle memory and timing.

Learning to be a good field shooter is like learning to play golf. First you must learn the swing. Before you can hope to be successful you must understand the principles involved and have a mental image of what a good swing looks like. This is relatively easy for the golfer. There are any number of good books available to help him, and he can easily enlist the aid of a pro. But little has been written about shotgun swing as it pertains to the field. Many books deal with hunting, with selection of guns, chokes, and loads, and there are several good books on skeet and trap shooting technique. But there are relatively few dealing with shooting technique as it pertains to the field. It is even more difficult to find a pro to help with your swing.

In this chapter, I will describe what I believe are the components of a good shotgun swing. Like all sports, there is room for individuality. If you analyzed the golf swing of the top ten money winners on the PGA Tour, you would find they all have their own styles. But you would also find that there were many things in common. The same is true of good field shooters. They all have their own styles, but there are common denominators. I have been using the term swing, but "gun mount" might be better used to describe the shotgunner's motion. For a field shooter the gun mount and swing blend into one. A skeet or trap shooter

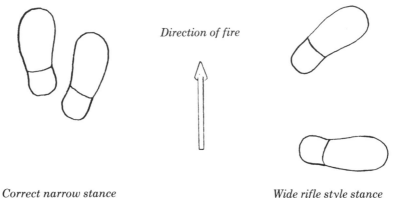

Correct narrow stance   *Direction of fire*   *Wide rifle style stance*

mounts his gun as a preliminary action, and his swing is a separate entity. I will discuss gun mount and swing as one, as I believe they should be for a field gunner.

The technique preached by the British is based on our natural ability to point. Reduced to its simplest elements, the system requires a shooter to use a properly fit gun, use correct gun-mounting technique or a good swing, and to keep his eye on the bird. The necessity of keeping your eye on the bird has already been dealt with. Gun fit will be considered in a subsequent chapter. Let's analyze the swing.

STANCE

Let's begin our discussion with the feet and work up. A good wing shot keeps his feet as close together as possible while maintaining good balance. If the footing is good and the terrain level, the heels should be no more than 6 inches apart. The left foot should be pointed in the anticipated direction of fire and slightly ahead of the right foot.* The right foot will be toed-out slightly. If the left foot is at twelve o'clock, the right foot would be pointing at two o'clock. If the feet were brought together, the ball of the right foot would meet the arch of the left.

It is important to keep the shoulders and hips square to the direction of fire. Your belly button should be pointing in the same direction as

* Throughout this discussion I will adopt the view of a right-handed shooter. If you are a lefty, just reverse my right and left designations.

A narrow stance will allow a shooter to pivot freely and keep the shoulders level and head erect.

the gun. Your initial stance should have you facing in the anticipated direction of fire. If the target swings right or left, you must be able to turn the entire body in order to remain square with the target. If you can maintain this orientation to the target, the left hand will naturally point your gun where your eyes are looking. A narrow stance will allow the shooter to pivot freely and keep his shoulders and hips moving together. Proper footwork will allow you to swing your gun easily through at least a 180-degree arc without losing your balance or moving your feet. Pivoting on a narrow base will help keep your shoulders level and your head steady as you turn. It is most important for a shooter to minimize head motion. If the shooter's eye is held steady, it is relatively easy for him to instinctively point out his target. If the head and eye are in motion as he points, the formula for alignment becomes very complicated. Try it; consciously move your head to the side as you attempt to point at an object—tough, isn't it? Now, hold your head steady and point—much easier.

Wing shooting is by no means unique in this regard. Steadying the head makes any eye–hand activity easier. Watch a good golfer or baseball player as they swing; or better yet, look at sequential photographs of either's swing. You will find there is an absolute minimum of head motion. When swinging a shotgun, the part of your anatomy farthest from your head has a great effect on how steady you hold it. The position of your feet will determine, to a large extent, the stability of the head during the swing.

American shooters typically adopt too wide a stance. A wide stance increases the tendency to lean. With the feet held apart it is nearly impossible to pivot—one lacks the narrow base necessary to do so. The wide stance prevents the hips from moving with the shoulders, because the wide base holds the hips in a near-fixed position. As the shooter tries to swing right or left, the upper body leans and the head drops. Most frequently, the wide stance will cause the shoulder nearest the direction of rotation to be pulled down. That is, if the shooter is attempting a left-to-right crossing shot, his right shoulder will dip as he turns. As his right shoulder drops, his head will be pulled down with it. The most common miss in a crossing target at medium to long range is low and behind. Often this miss can be traced directly to a stance that is too wide.

The American predilection for a wide stance is yet another side effect of our rifle bias. Spreading the feet and dropping the shooting shoulder back is fine if your target is stationary. This stance gives good stability, but it is not flexible enough for something as dynamic as wing shooting. With the correct narrow stance, the hips and shoulders can move together. This pivoting motion allows the shooter to keep his shoulders

A wide stance will force a shooter to lean and drop his head.

level and his head erect. This swing will help the shooter keep his eye steady and make his gun point more naturally.

READY POSITION

Whenever possible, a shooter should come to a ready or alert position prior to attempting the gun mount. If we have one standard starting position it will be easier for us to groove the swing, to duplicate the gun mount time after time. If we are ever to become good field shots the gun must be brought into the shoulder and cheek in such a fashion that the eye is placed in the proper relationship to the barrels (see the Gun Fit chapter). Use of a standardized starting position will make it easier to develop the muscle memory necessary to be consistent with the gun mount.

Most wing shooters are totally oblivious of their starting positions. After a shot they probably can't tell you what position their gun was in when they swung into action. As they begin one shot the gun is over the shoulder, at the next it is held at port arms and on the third it is straight up. The variety in starting position complicates the swing. The muscle pattern required to move the gun from over the shoulder to the shooting position is very different from the muscle pattern moving it from port arms to shooting position. Why learn several different swings, when if we eliminated the variety in the initial position, we could use just one?

The field gunner does not enjoy much control over his environment. We do not know when a bird will flush, in most cases. We cannot maintain one gun attitude throughout a long day in the field. But if you have the time, and the warning, get your gun into a standard ready, or alert position. If you are caught by surprise, make every effort to come to your ready for an instant just prior to mounting the gun to shoulder.

Some types of shooting lend themselves better to the ready position than others. It is certainly easier to use a standard ready position on a European-style driven shoot than a walkup shoot. Shooting quail, woodcock, or ruffed grouse in heavy cover makes it difficult to standardize your starting position, but if you can train yourself to ready the gun momentarily before making the move to shoulder, you will be a better shot. This is easier said than done. When a quail or grouse bursts out from under your feet, it takes a shooter of unusually steady nerve not to snap the gun immediately to shoulder. And if you ever get so blasé as *not* to be unnerved by a bird roaring out unexpectedly, you should probably quit hunting!

Of the over two thousand students I have worked with, almost every

A good ready or alert position.

one of them could cite a case in which a ready position was not easily used. I agree; there are many shooting situations where adopting a standard ready position is difficult, or nearly impossible. Do the best you can. Just because it is difficult to do in a particular situation is not justification for scrapping the technique. In many situations coming to the ready is easy, and it will help your swing no matter what the degree of difficulty may be in getting to it. What we are trying to do is simplify the swing or gun mount. No matter how tough it may be to get to the ready, it will make everything easier from that point on. It is what happens after the ready has been assumed that is critical.

What is the best ready position? The gun must be held in a safe manner, and in an attitude that will minimize the difficulty in bringing it to shoulder, a position that will not obstruct the shooter's field of vision nor distract visually from his target, and one that will accentuate his natural pointing instinct. Most people will find that a ready position like that in the illustration on page 13 will work best. The heel of the stock should be tucked just under the shooting arm and drawn up to the underarm. The muzzle should be at eye level and right in front of the shooter's face. About one and a half or two inches of the stock should be caught under the arm. If the stock is pulled further back under the arm the motion is unnecessarily complicated. If less, or none, of the stock is under the arm, the stock may come to the cheek before the lead hand has had a chance to naturally point the barrels at the target.

Our entire technique is based on our natural ability to point. We must use a gun mount that will accentuate our natural pointing instinct. Point at something. Now carefully analyze what you did. Your hand with outstretched finger did not come straight up in front of your eye. You pushed your hand out more than you raised it. This is what we should do with our shotgun if we are to best utilize our natural

*The muzzles should be held directly in front
of the shooter in the ready position.*

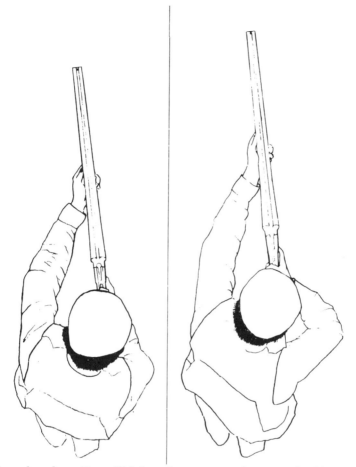

A good ready position will help a shooter mount the gun to shoulder properly.

instinct. By burying an inch and a half or two of the stock under the arm, the gun is prevented from being pulled straight up. We are forced to push the gun out as though we were pointing.

The lead hand (left hand for a right-handed shooter) does the point-ing. We want to position the lead hand so that it will move with a natural pointing gesture. Point at something again. Now look at the position of the hand and arm you are pointing with. Your hand is well out in front of your face, and your arm is nearly extended. That is the natural pointing attitude and that is where your lead hand should be when the gun is shouldered. Carefully place your gun on your shoulder so that the heel of the stock is level with the top of your shoulder. Now

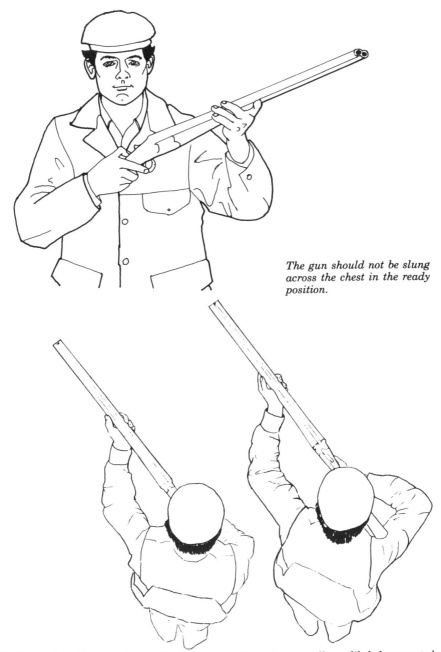

The gun should not be slung across the chest in the ready position.

If the gun is held across the chest in the ready position, the gun will very likely be mounted to the arm rather than the shoulder.

put your left hand out in a natural pointing position and place the barrels in your left hand. Slip the gun off your shoulder and pull the heel of the stock under your arm an inch and a half. Lower the muzzles to eye level, and keep them right off the end of your nose. You've got it; a nice, ready position. From this starting position you can push the gun forward and up to shoulder and cheek with an economy of motion that utilizes your natural pointing instincts.

Be careful that your ready position does not sling the gun across your chest. It is most important that the muzzles be in front of your nose, not your left shoulder (presuming you are a right-handed shooter). If the gun is allowed to lie across the chest it will give the shooter a tendency to mount the stock out on his arm. This will make him shoot across his line of vision. A right-hander will shoot left. In the ready position the gun should be held as close as possible to 90 degrees to the line of the shoulders. This will help keep the stock in on the shoulder and minimize the tendency to shoot left.

The fingers of the lead hand must be spread out enough so that they do not come over the top of the barrels. If they do, it will partially obscure the line of sight or, even if not, be visually distracting. The gun should be held firmly, but not with a white-knuckle grip. The

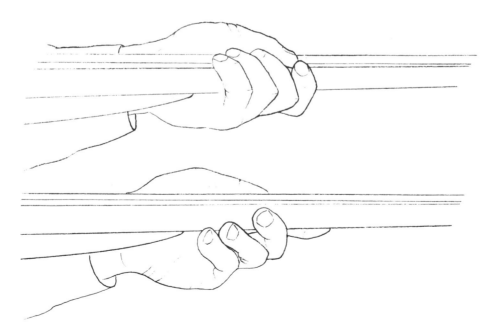

The fingers of the lead hand must be spread out enough so that they do not wrap over the top of the barrels.

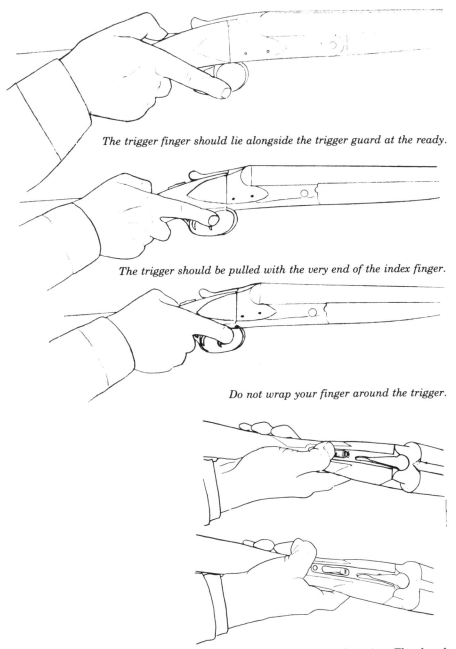

The trigger finger should lie alongside the trigger guard at the ready.

The trigger should be pulled with the very end of the index finger.

Do not wrap your finger around the trigger.

The thumb should push across a top tang safety with a diagonal motion. The thumb should wrap around the stock after the safety has been disengaged.

fingers of the right hand should wrap aroung the wrist of the stock with the trigger finger outstretched and lying along the side of the trigger guard. Never place your finger on the trigger in the ready position. The trigger finger should not contact the trigger until the last instant when the gun is fired. The trigger should be pulled with the very end of the index finger. Do not wrap your finger around the trigger so that the knuckle is past the trigger. You have the best feel for a trigger when you use just the fleshy tip of your finger.

If you are using a breaking gun or any gun with a top tang safety, the thumb of the trigger hand should be on the safety. The thumb should push across the safety with a diagonal motion. A right-handed shooter pushes his thumb from right to left as it moves forward and continues that motion after the safety has been disengaged. The right thumb ends up being wrapped around the wrist of the stock. Do not leave the thumb on top of the safety, particularly if you are shooting a breaking gun with top lever. Recoil can jam your thumb into the top lever and give you an unforgettably sore thumb. If your gun is equipped with a trigger-guard safety, you should put the tip of your trigger finger on the safety in the ready position. After the safety has been pushed off, the finger moves to the trigger.

No matter what style of safety you are using, there is no reason to

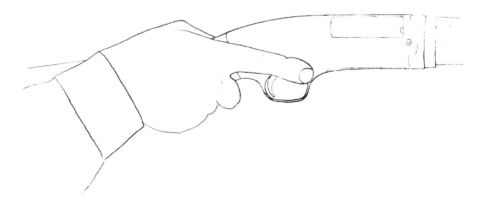

If using a trigger guard safety, the tip of the index finger should rest on the safety in the ready position.

disengage it until your gun actually starts toward the shoulder. I do not condone a safety being clicked off prior to the gun mount in any hunting situation. Removing the safety should be part of the gun-mount reflex. You will not save one milisecond by taking it off as a preliminary to the gun mount.

TIMING AND MOTION

You are in the ready position and a bird flushes. Now what? The very first thing a shooter must do is make visual contact with the target. Don't try to shoot it until you can see it. This may sound ridiculous, but believe me, most shooters try to bring the gun fully to shoulder before they are visually locked on the target. I have watched shooters on a quail walk raise their guns to shoulder and point in a direction that had no relation to the flight of the target being launched. The explanation was always "I thought it was going over there." Shooting is an eye–hand activity that should be automatic, without having to think about it. The circuitry should be straight from eye to hand. If you route things through the gray matter, you'll probably miss.

Why does a shooter so frequently raise gun to shoulder before he has seen the target? In many walk-up shooting situations you hear a bird before you see it. The shooter is over-anxious and snaps the gun up to shoulder. He must then try to locate the bird and swing the gun in the proper direction. This shooter has thrown away his natural pointing instincts to a large extent. He must try to locate the bird with the gun barrels right in the middle of his field of vision. It is difficult not to be distracted by the barrels. Secondly, he has thrown away the natural pointing gesture that we all have. He used it up before his eye had focused on his target. He might just as well close his eyes while raising his gun to shoulder.

An experienced field shooter will find his target before he shoulders his gun. Your ear certainly helps your eye to get your initial bearing, but a good field shooter does not actually raise his gun to shoulder until his eye has made contact with the bird. It is during this split second, when the bird is heard but not yet seen, that an experienced gunner comes to the ready position. He will also instinctively turn his body to face in the direction the bird is flying. This initial alignment is, many times, done almost exclusively by ear. The key is that the gun is not put to shoulder until the eye is locked on the target. We cannot possibly use our pointing instincts to best advantage if we don't have our eyes locked on first.

Slow down. The hand is quicker than the eye. Give your eye a chance to find the bird. All too often I've watched a shooter snap a gun to

Come to the ready position just prior to mounting the gun.

The gun should slip out from under the arm and come up to meet the underside of the shooter's cheekbone.

shoulder like a flyweight boxer throwing a jab. Unfortunately, after the blur of motion that is their gun mount, the shooter usually slams on the breaks, then attempts to align bird and barrel with jerky little motions. This hop and stop technique is seldom successful. A good shooter should be smooth. A good wing shooter should look like he is dancing a Viennese waltz, not sparring with Sugar Ray Leonard. A gun that starts quickly will usually stop quickly. If you can start your gun moving slowly you will be well on your way to developing a smooth, continuous swing.

Relax. You cannot move smoothly if your body is rigid. You must be visually sharp, but you cannot afford to allow this visual acuity to translate itself into a white-knuckle grip and a tensing of every muscle in your body. Again, the analogy to other eye–hand sports is obvious. To be successful at any eye–hand activity, you must be able to bear down visually without tensing.

Your stance is narrow, you have come to a good ready position, you have locked your eye on the target and you have instinctively turned to face your target. What next? The lead hand (left hand for a right-handed shooter) should push the gun into shooting position and simultaneously and instinctively point the target out. The trigger hand helps push the gun to shoulder, but it is the lead hand that should do

Most of us have a little too much neck to be anatomically-ideal shooting machines. If the head does not move forward the eye is held too high above the line of the barrels.

The manner in which the head moves is extremely critical. The head should move ever so slightly forward.

most of the work. The gun should slip out from under the arm and come up to meet the underside of the shooter's cheekbone. Head motion should be held to a minimum, as discussed earlier. Ideally, the head would remain perfectly steady and the gun would come all the way up to meet the cheek. For all but a very few, this is difficult to do. Most shooters have to drop thier head slightly to attain the proper relationship of eye to barrel. If they hold their head perfectly still the eye is placed too high over the barrel, and they will shoot over the top of their targets. Most of us have a little too much neck to be anatomically ideal shooting machines.

The manner in which we move our heads is extremely critical. The head should move ever so slightly forward. This motion lowers our eye with a minimum adverse effect on our natural pointing abilities. If a stock were designed to accomodate the length of our necks in an upright posture, we would have so much drop that the gun would tend to recoil up into our cheeks. (See the chapter on Gun Fit). The compromise is to design a comfortable stock that will require a minimum of head motion. It is extremely important that the head motion not be lateral. Many a new shooter tries to tip his head to the side to bring his eye into alignment with the barrels. This tendency adversely affects the natural ability to point. It also makes the recoil felt at the cheek most unpleasant.

The gun should slip out from under the arm, where it has been held

Do not tip the head to the side as the gun is mounted.

at ready, and move up and forward until the stock is in firm contact with the underside of the cheekbone. What about the shoulder? All but real tyros know that the shoulder and butt of the stock should be held firmly together to minimize the discomfort of recoil. If the gun is held away from the shoulder the recoil will be much sharper. The key is to bring the shoulder forward to meet the gun, rather than pulling the gun back to the shoulder. The heel of the stock should slide up the face of the shoulder as the gun is mounted. As the gun comes into the cheek the shoulder is rolled slightly forward in a sort of shrugging motion. This snugs the shoulder and stock together and minimizes recoil. The heel of the stock should be level with the top of the shoulder. The butt should be just outside of the high part of the collarbone, but not out on the arm. This proper placement on the shoulder is made easier by a good ready position.

The gun must not be pulled back to meet the shoulder because this interrupts the natural flow of the shot. The weight should move with the target. If the initial stance is good and the shooter is standing up straight, weight will shift in the direction the target is moving, following the motion of the left hand and gun. The pointing hand will create a subtle shift of weight in the direction the target is moving. If the gun is pulled back to the shoulder, this natural weight shift is interrupted. As the gun is pulled back there is a tendency to shift the weight back. A shooter who pulls his gun back into his shoulder will usually shift

It is important to lean into the shot. The weight should be on the balls of the feet.

his weight onto his rear foot (right foot for a right-hander). This weight
shift will make the muzzles rise, and in most cases one will shoot over
the top of the bird. Rolling the shoulder into the gun accentuates the
natural weight shift. In the ready position, the weight should be slightly
forward favoring the ball of the left foot. You want to lean into the
shot. Balance is better and one moves more smoothly if the weight is
on the balls of the feet. Pulling the gun back shifts weight to the heels.

The most important thing of all is to keep your eyes on the bird
when you pull the trigger. You should never be visually conscious of
your gun. The gun should move in one smooth motion from your ready
position to shoulder and cheek, and the shot should be taken immediately. Do not look down to the gun to check your alignment (see
Chapter 3). If there is any magic in the formula, it is in the eye. In its

Do not sit back on your heels as you shoot.

marvelous ability to direct our hand straight to the object at which we are looking, it does it without any conscious thought process. The single most important element in the whole process is visual concentration. At the instant we pull the trigger our eye must be focused on the bird, not the barrel.

It is important that the shot be taken as soon as the gun is shouldered. The longer the gun is held in the fully-shouldered position, the more likely the shooter will be distracted by the gun. Shoot with your first attempt. The gun mount and swing must be smooth and fluid, but we must be ready to shoot as soon as we make that last little push with the lead hand.

Many times I have seen shooters deteriorate as they began to over-think a shot. A student is given a new shot—a target thrown at a different angle and range than those he has been practicing. As instructor I discuss with the students the techniques they should be conscious of as they shoot this target. Usually, I just review basic things, like proper stance, smooth gun mount, and visual concentration. Typically the student will respond to the new angle and range beautifully and break the first two or three targets. But it is not unusual for students then to go into a little slump, and miss two or three. The first few they shoot instinctively, allowing their eye and hand to work together. They had no preconceived notion of where the target was going. They were relaxed because this was something new and if they missed, well, what the heck. After breaking the first few they begin to tense a little and overthink the shot.

A subtle timing change is the tip-off to what is happening. The student shoots the first few targets as soon as the gun comes into the cheek. As he begins to think too much and tense a bit his response to the trigger is slowed. Typically, there is no perceptible change in the motion, but the gun is held on the shoulder just a little too long before the shot is taken. A good field gunner must shoot confidently with one smooth motion. If he tries to bring the gun to shoulder and then ride the bird as he double checks alignment, the natural pointing instinct will be lost.

People often have stories about great shots they have known. Some of them more preposterous than others, but many have a common thread. Whether the great shot was in the marsh or upland he is frequently described as a shooter who "just pulled up and fired." This statement is made as further testimony to how great this individual really was, in a tone that implies, "Think how good he might have been if he took a second to really make sure after having mounted the gun." In fact it was the great shot's timing that contributed largely to his success. He was a seasoned veteran and had developed the confidence to shoot with one fluid motion. Don't try to second guess. Move the gun smoothly to cheek and shoulder, keep your eye on the bird, and shoot without hesitation.

The concept of getting the gun and body moving with the target before the gun is fully mounted is an important one. The swing and the gun mount are integrated. Unfortunately most shooters seem naturally inclined to segregate the gun mount and the swing. They will usually mount the gun fully to cheek and shoulder before starting to move, or swing, with the target. This, like many of our shotgunning problems, can be traced to early rifle training. The rifleman mounts his gun and then aligns his sights. They are two distinct operations. A shotgunner on the trap or skeet field likewise segregates gun mount from alignment. The field gunner must learn to move with the target from the first moment he sees it. He starts his swing before his gun mount in many instances. Crossing shots are most demanding in this regard. If a shooter will learn to begin the lateral motion necessary to keep him square with the target before he starts the gun up to shoulder, he will find crossing shots much easier. If the shoulders and hips are turned to keep the shooter facing his bird as the gun is mounted, he will have a natural momentum to his swing. It is this natural momentum that we depend on to keep us moving through our target. The question of lead will be dealt with in a separate chapter. Suffice it to say for now that if we can learn to integrate our swing and gun mount everything will flow more naturally.

4

Gun Fit

The English shooting technique requires the use of a properly fit gun. The gun must be designed so that when it is brought to shoulder and cheek properly it will naturally point where the shooter is looking. We presume that the shooter has sufficient eye–hand coordination to point. We also presume that the shooter will practice gun mounting until he is able to bring the gun to shoulder and cheek properly. Gun mounting is discussed in Chapter 3 on Basic Technique. Let's consider what is meant by a properly fit gun.

A shotgun should be designed so that the eye will naturally align with the barrel. The size and shape of the stock should be determined by the physique of the shooter. Field shooting dictates that the gun be brought to shoulder with one smooth motion and the shot be taken without hesitation. There is no time to adjust the gun on the shoulder and cheek to insure that the eye is properly aligned. The stock should therefore be proportioned to the shooter. One size does not fit all, but unfortunately most guns are sold with only one size stock. This is an unfortunate but unavoidable outgrowth of mass-produced guns. Fire-arms manufacturers cannot afford to produce and warehouse several different stock sizes. If they did, the price of our shotguns would jump dramatically. The gun manufacturers produce a standard size stock that they feel will fit their typical gun customer. The hypothetical Mr. Average is usually five-feet nine-inches tall, weighs approximately 165 pounds and wears a forty regular suit. If this sounds familiar, you may be one of those lucky people who can pick up most standard-stock guns and shoot them quite well. The more you deviate from this norm the more you may benefit from a custom stock or from modifying a standard stock.

29

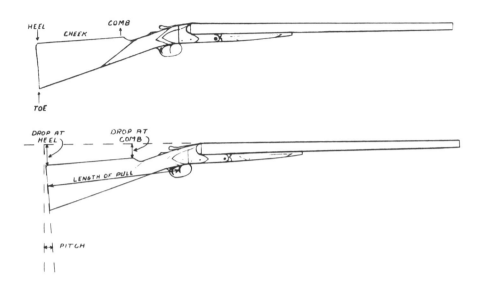

Proper alignment of the eye with the barrel is not only consideration when fitting a stock. The stock must be designed to make the gun comfortable to shoot. The size and shape of the stock cannot affect the force of the recoil other than by the degree to which it adds weight, but the design of the stock can influence how comfortable the gun is to shoot. We want to minimize discomfort. The gun should be designed to distribute the recoil as evenly as possible.

How does a gun fitter go about achieving these ends of proper eye alignment and minimum recoil discomfort? When fitting a stock to a shooter a gun fitter should use a try gun. This gun has an adjustable stock that can be tailored to the individual. The illustrations above provide the nomenclature generally used to describe the parts of a gun stock and show the stock measurements taken when a stock is fit.

By having an individual fire a try gun at a stationary target with a solid background the fitter can tailor the stock to the individual. The fitter watches as the individual fire's the try gun and is able to look at the stationary target and see exactly where the shot struck. The target, generally a small metal bull's eye, is placed on a large metal plate that has been painted white, allowing the fitter to see exactly where the shot landed. By adjusting the stock the fitter adjusts the alignment of the shooter's eye relative to the barrel. By adjusting the stock we can make the gun point naturally at the spot where the shooter is looking.

Try gun with adjustable stock used for fitting.

Try gun and stationary target.

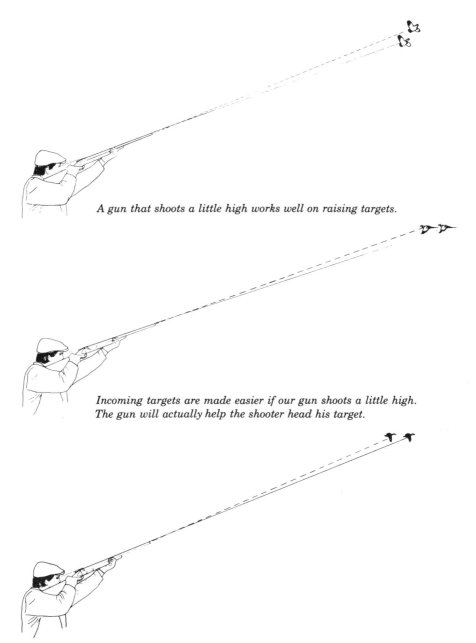

A gun that shoots a little high works well on raising targets.

Incoming targets are made easier if our gun shoots a little high. The gun will actually help the shooter head his target.

An overhead bird that is going away is made more difficult to hit with a gun that shoots high. The occasions where a moderately high-shooting gun are a benefit seem to outweigh those where it is a hindrance.

In essence, the shooter's eye is used like the rear sight on a rifle. We move the eye by stock dimension changes, whereas the rifleman moves his sight. We are creating a stock that, if properly mounted, will put the shooter's master eye slightly above the line of the barrel, but centered left and right. We want a field gun to shoot just a little high at typical range. This will allow the shooter to keep the bird in full view as he is shooting. If we did not position the shooter's eye slightly above the line of the rib, the shooter would be forced to bring the barrels directly between his eye and his bird and partially obscure his target. This tends to distract the shooter and break concentration on the bird. The natural pointing response actually brings the pointer, whether it be finger or gun, just under the object at which we are looking. Try it: point at something quickly. You will not obscure your view of the object you are pointing at by bringing your finger directly between your eye and the object. The finger will typically be brought just beneath the object. Couple this with the fact that in most field situations a little rising lead is helpful and the reason for making our field gun shoot a little high becomes apparent. If we are walk-up shooting, typically birds flush and are rising as we shoot. A gun that shoots just a little high will make the shot more natural. When pass shooting, where birds are coming in overhead, the rising lead becomes a built-in lead and works to our advantage. Guns used exclusively for European-style driven shoots are many times built to shoot very high for this reason. There are certain occasions when the rising lead works against us. Trying to shoot a high bird that is going away from us is one. Here the rising lead puts us behind. All and all the occasions when the rising lead is a benefit seem to outweigh those occasions when it is detrimental.

Our field gun should shoot just a little high. It should come to shoulder easily and smoothly, and it should distribute the recoil as evenly as possible to minimize discomfort. Let's consider each of the stock measurements and how it typically affects one's shooting.

LENGTH OF PULL

Most shooters are familiar with this measurement. It is the distance from the middle of the trigger to the middle of the stock's butt. This distance affects the shooter in several ways. First, it will determine to a large extent where the shooter's cheek will meet the stock. The greater the pull dimension, the further back on the stock the cheek will fall. In my opinion, the cheek should meet the stock just forward of the midpoint between heel and comb.

Length of pull is determined by the length of the shooter's arm, his

The cheek should meet the stock just ahead of the midpoint between heel and comb.

general physique (slim or heavy), and the degree to which the shooter thrusts his head forward as he mounts the gun. Generally speaking, the longer the arm, the slimmer the build, and the more the shooter pushes his head forward, the longer the stock must be. The old technique of placing the butt stock in the crook of the elbow and extending the index finger to the trigger to determine length of pull is better than nothing, but not really adequate. This test for determining length of pull does not take into account the chest size, general muscular development, and gun-mounting style. By using a try gun with an adjustable length of pull, a gun fitter can take into account all the idiosyncrasies of the shooter's physique and style.

Not only does the length of pull affect the location of the cheek on the stock and thereby the relationships of eye to barrel, but length of pull is also the primary determinant of the gun's ease of mounting. If the stock is of the proper length the gun will come to shoulder smoothly with a minimum of seesawing. If the stock is too long it will be difficult to get the gun to shoulder without the heel catching under the shooter's armpit. The barrels will have a tendency to come up ahead of the stock and the shooter will miss high.

The old technique to determine length of pull: place the butt stock in the crook of the elbow and extend the index finger to the trigger. This method is better than nothing, but not really adequate.

A stock that is too long may also cause a shooter to mount the butt stock out on his bicep rather than into the shoulder. With the butt stock on the bicep the recoil is most unpleasant and the shooter will have a tendency to crossfire. That is, a right-handed shooter will shoot left and a lefty will miss to the right. A high bird that is coming directly overhead brings out this tendency to crossfire in many shooters. A right-handed shooter will almost never miss this high-incoming target on the right side. If a windage error is made it will almost invariably be to the left. This tendency of the righty to shoot left is usually a product of an improper gun mount, and the poor gun mount is many times linked to a stock that is too long.

If the stock is too short the shooter's cheek will be placed too close to the comb. In the extreme case the thumb of the trigger hand may

If the stock is too long it will be difficult to get the gun to shoulder without the heel catching under the shooter's arm.

A stock that is too long may cause a shooter to mount the butt stock on his bicep rather than into the shoulder.

actually hit the shooter in the nose when the gun is fired. A stock that is too short will also tend to come to shoulder too fast. The stock will many times come to cheek before the barrels are aligned. This will give the shooter a tendency to shoot low.

Generally speaking, it is easier to cope with a stock that is a little short rather than one that is a little long. Of course we hope our stock will be exactly the right length, but many times that is more difficult to achieve than would seem the case. Effective length of pull is determined by more than just the length of the stock. The type of clothing you wear directly affects length of pull. If you are a one-gun shooter and use the same gun for both upland and waterfowl gunning, you will in all likelihood be dealing with different lengths of pull. During the warm part of the upland season you will probably be wearing a medium-weight canvas shirt and a light vest. If you are a dove hunter, the opening day may find you in little more than a tee-shirt. By the end of the waterfowl season, you will probably pile on every piece of clothing you own short of your bathrobe as you try to ward off the icy winds. The shotgun clutched in your frozen fingers may look familiar but when those late season blue bills come barreling in and you try to bring the gun to shoulder, it feels strange. Is it any wonder the gun that once felt so natural now wants to hang up under your arm? By the time you

If the stock is too short the thumb of the trigger hand may hit the shooter's nose when the gun is fired.

factor in all those layers of clothes your real length of pull has increased tremendously. Ideally we would have two guns with the length of pull tailored to the type of clothing we will be wearing. Short of that, and assuming you are as avid a duck hunter as you are an upland gunner, determine length of pull while wearing the clothes you normally use for your cold-weather shooting. This will make your stock a little short for your early season gunning, but better that than vice-versa.

You can make a gun feel longer or shorter by changing the position of your lead hand (left hand for a right-handed shooter). Normally, the lead hand should be placed far enough out on the forearm or barrels so that the arm will be nearly straight when the gun is shouldered. (See Chapter 3). By moving the lead hand back the gun will feel shorter; if we move the hand forward the gun will feel longer. This adjustment of the lead hand cannot correct for a grossly illfit stock. There is no substitute for a stock of the correct length, but by adjusting our lead-hand position we can compensate somewhat for the difference in length of pull created by different amounts of clothing.

Most shotguns designed for field use will be made with 14- or 14¼-inch lengths of pull. This length works well for our Mr. Average. He hypothetically is 5'9" or 5'10", has a sleeve length of 33 inches and wears a 40 regular suit. Most people of this size will find a 14- or 14¼-inch length of pull quite comfortable. However, if you are not a Mr. Average, the 14-inch length of pull may be a burden. A shooter standing 5'2" can't comfortably deal with a 14-inch stock. If you are 6'2" you obviously may not find a 14-inch length of pull ideal either. I wish I could give you a formula for computing length of pull based on your height, but unfortunately there are too many variables to allow for this type of solution. There is no substitute for a knowledgable gun fitter and an adjustable stock try gun.

DROP AT COMB

This is the distance between the top of the barrels or rib and the top of the stock at the comb. You can easily take this measurement on your own guns by placing the gun upside down on a flat surface. With the top of the receiver and the barrel or rib against the top of a table or other flat surface measure the distance from the comb of the stock to the table top. Be careful that the bead or beads hang over the edge of the table. If the bead rests on the table it will give you a false measurement.

Drop at comb is the principal determinant of how high or low the gun will shoot. Even small variations in this measurement will create

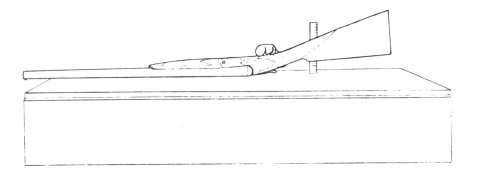

Measuring drop at comb.

a marked difference in the way the gun will shoot. The shooter's cheek should contact the stock just a few inches behind the comb. Changing the drop at comb by as little as ⅛-inch will have a perceptible effect on how high the gun shoots. Most shotgun stocks produced for field and for skeet shooting will have a drop at comb of 1½ inches. This measurement will work very well for many shooters. The overwhelming majority of field-style shooters can be accommodated by a variation as slight as 1¼ to 1¾ inches. Trap shooters many times favor stocks that have little drop at comb; the same holds true for some live-pigeon or driven-bird enthusiasts. The idiosyncrises of these shooters' styles may be complemented by a gun with very little drop. I am confining my discussion to the needs of the field shooter, and it is my belief that the field shooter who needs less than 1¼ or more than 1¾ inches of drop at comb is exceedingly rare.

The amount of drop at comb is determined primarily by the distance from the underside of the cheek bone to the center of the eye. The amount of drop will also be affected by how firmly the shooter checks his gun. The more firmly the stock is checked the less drop at comb required. If we increase the drop at comb we lower the eye relative to the barrels; by decreasing drop we of course raise the eye. If we increase drop and lower the eye a shooter using the instinctive field technique will shoot lower. Decreasing drop at comb has the opposite effect. When fitting a stock for field shooting we want the eye just above the rib or top of the barrel.

Typically a tall person with a long face will need greater drop at

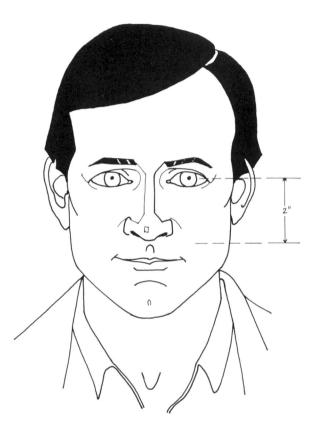

The amount of drop required is determined primarily by the distance from the underside of the shooter's cheekbone to the center of the eye.

comb than a small, round-faced individual. But no matter how long and tall or how short and squatty, there is not a tremendous variation in the distance between peoples' eyes and cheek bones.

DROP AT HEEL

This is the distance between the top of the barrels or rib and the top of the stock at the heel. This measurement can be taken via the same procedure used for measuring drop at comb. Drop at heel also affects how high a gun will shoot. It is the combined effects of drop at comb

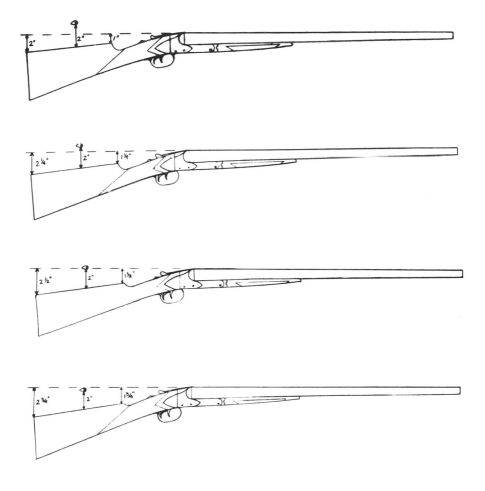

The combined effects of drop at comb and drop at heel determine the height of the eye relative to the rib or barrel.

and heel that determines the height of the eye relative to the rib or barrel. The higher the eye is held the higher the gun will tend to shoot. The principal determinants of drop at heel are the length of the shooter's neck and the degree to which he pushes his head forward as the gun is mounted.

Most shotguns designed for field shooting are produced with stocks that have 2½ inches of drop at the heel. This, combined with the standard comb dimension of 1½ inches, will work well for Mr. Average. The stock has been designed for our hypothetical 5'9", 165-pound male shooter. Barring any unusual physical traits or peculiar gun-mounting techniques these drops usually work very nicely. If a shooter has a long neck and holds his head very erect as he shoots a little more drop at heel may help him. Conversely, a short-necked sort may need a little less. In my experience a field shooter seldom benefits from a drop of less than 2 inches or more than 2¾ inches at the heel. As with drop at comb, the variation in drop at heel is not large in terms of inches, but the effect of a ⅛- or ¼-inch can be tremendous in a shooter's success.

When fitting a stock to a shooter, we are trying to place the eye behind the barrels in such a fashion that the gun naturally points where the individual is looking. We also must be mindful of the manner in which the gun will recoil. In this regard it is important to keep the drop at comb and drop at heel in balance. That is, that there not be too great a difference between the two measurements. If the difference between drops at comb and heel exceeds an inch, the gun will have a tendency to jump. The greater the difference between drop at comb and drop at heel the more the recoil will be felt in the cheek. The angle

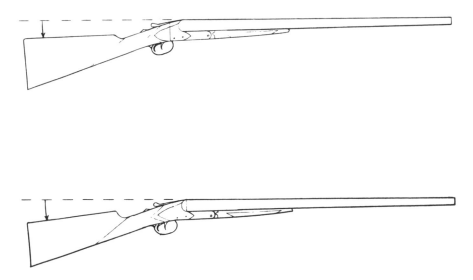

The greater the difference between drop at comb and drop at heel the more the recoil will be felt in the cheek. The angle formed between the top of the stock and the barrels should be held to a minimum and still place the shooter's eye in the proper position.

formed between the top of the stock and the barrels should be held to a minimum and still place the shooter's eye in the proper position. A stock dimension that works well for many people of average build is 1⅝ inches at the comb and 2¼ or 2⅜ inches at the heel. This places the eye at almost exactly the same height relative to the barrels as the standard 1½ × 2½-inch dimensions. The advantage of lowering the comb and raising the heel is to reduce the amount of recoil felt at the cheek.

The principle of reducing the angle formed between the top of the stock and the barrels can be taken to an extreme as far as the field shooter is concerned. Some shotguns used for trap shooting are designed with drops at comb and heel that are the same, i.e., 1½ inches at the comb and 1½ inches at the heel. These guns are generally pleasant to shoot in terms of recoil at the cheek, but most field shooters would shoot over the top of most of their birds. The trap shooter's technique has been specially tailored to harmonize with this type of stock. A trap shooters' environment is very controlled by field standards and allows a shooter to build in the necessary compensation. A field shooter using an instinctive pointing technique would find it difficult to use this trap stock. The eye is held well over the line of the barrels and gives the shooter a tendency to shoot high.

A field stock should have enough drop to place the eye just over the line of the barrel or rib. For most people the distance from the center of the eye to the underside of the cheekbone is about 2 inches. It is no accident that a stock with 1½-inch drop at comb and 2½-inch at heel will have about 2 inches of drop at a point midway between these points. This is what is called drop at cheek. Why not just make the drop 2 inches all the way across and eliminate the angle that tends to make the gun recoil into the cheek? The reason we make the heel drop greater than the comb is to place the gun more solidly on the shoulder. The shoulder is slightly lower than the cheek when we are in shooting position. A stock with a little extra drop at heel will come into the shoulder more naturally and better distribute the recoil on the shoulder.

CAST

Cast is the distance the gun stock is bent to the right or left relative to the barrels. The function of cast is to correct for any right or left alignment error. Just as drop is our elevation adjustment, cast is our windage adjustment. How much cast is required by a shooter is determined by the fullness of the face and the width of the shoulders. When a gun is brought to cheek, it does not always fall into perfect alignment with the eye. Most people find that their eye is held off

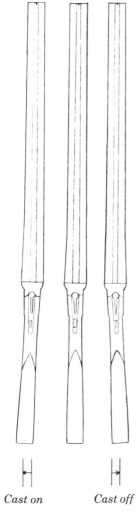

Cast on   Cast off

Cast is the distance the gun stock is bent to the right or left relative to the barrels.

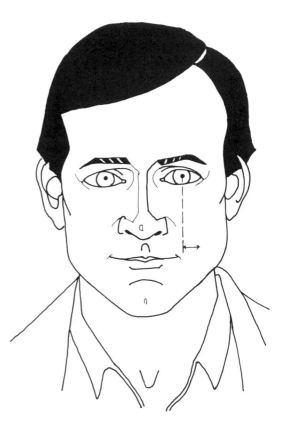

The principal determinant of the amount of cast required is the fullness of the face. People with broad faces may find that their eye is not directly above the spot where the stock contacts the cheek.

slightly to the side. A right-handed shooter will find that his eye is not directly behind the line of the barrels, but is off to the left a small amount (when viewed from behind). A person with a broad, full face generally has the greatest problem in this regard. His eye is not directly above the spot where the gun meets the underside of the cheekbone.

Casting bends the stock away from the shooter's face and allows his eye to move into direct alignment with the barrels. A right-handed shooter is given *cast off*. When the gun is viewed from behind the stock is to the right of the line of barrels.

Cast not only compensates for the relationship between eye and cheekbone, but also makes the butt stock fall more naturally into the shoulder. The butt stock should come into the shoulder without contacting the high portion of the collarbone. Broad-shouldered people sometimes find that when the gun is so positioned it is angled slightly across their faces. Looking at a right-handed shooter from behind we find that the gun is being pointed slightly to the left of the direction the shoulder is facing. By casting the stock we can achieve a more natural alignment of the gun with the direction of sight.

Most off-the-shelf guns are not cast because the manufacturers do not know whether the purchaser will be right- or left-handed. Nor do

When a gun is brought to cheek it does not always fall into perfect alignment with the eye. Here the shooter's eye is positioned slightly to the right of the rib.

Casting bends the stock away from the shooter's face and allows his eye to move into proper alignment with the rib and barrels.

they know how much cast would be required. Again we have the situation where a manufacturer is producing one gun to fit everyone. The most logical solution is not to bend the stock at all. Given the dilemma faced by gun manufacturers, they do a remarkably good job with their "Mr. Average" approach.

PITCH

This is the angle the butt stock is cut relative to the barrels. If the butt of the stock forms a 90-degree angle to the barrels this is considered 0 pitch. If the toe of the stock is cut back so that the angle formed between the barrels and the butt of the stock is less than 90 degrees, this is considered positive pitch. The pitch is measured in degrees from the right angle. A gun with +4 degrees of pitch would have a stock whose butt would form an angle of 86 degrees with the line of the barrels. A gun with −4 degrees of pitch would have a stock whose butt would form an angle of 94 degrees with the barrels.

Most guns designed for field use are given a small amount of positive pitch. The stock designed for Mr. Average will usually have +4 degrees of pitch. Varying the pitch of a stock will affect how recoil is distributed on the shoulder and, to a lesser extent, how high or low the gun will shoot. Let's consider the recoil aspect first. Most people find that when they have adapted a shooting position the shoulder and the chest area where the butt stock is placed does not form a 90-degree angle to the line of the barrels. The chest and pectoral muscles where the toe of the stock contact the shooter's body are seldom directly beneath the shoulder area where the heel of the stock rests. The area where the toe of the stock hits the chest is usually a little forward of the shoulder. If a stock is cut with 0-degree pitch the toe tends to push hard into the chest and the heel is held slightly away from the shoulder. The recoil is felt primarily through the toe of the stock and digs into the chest. By cutting the stock with a modest amount of positive pitch we can make the butt stock conform to the shape of the shoulder and chest more closely. This has the effect of distributing the recoil over the entire surface of the butt stock and makes the gun more comfortable to shoot. We have not affected the force with which the gun recoils, which is a function of the load we are shooting. But we *have* affected how the recoil is distributed. If the entire surface of the butt stock is in firm contact with the shoulder and chest, the recoil will be less apparent than if only a small part of the butt stock is transferring the energy to the shooter.

The shape of the shoulder and chest will determine the amount of pitch required. A barrel-chested, muscular individual will usually re-

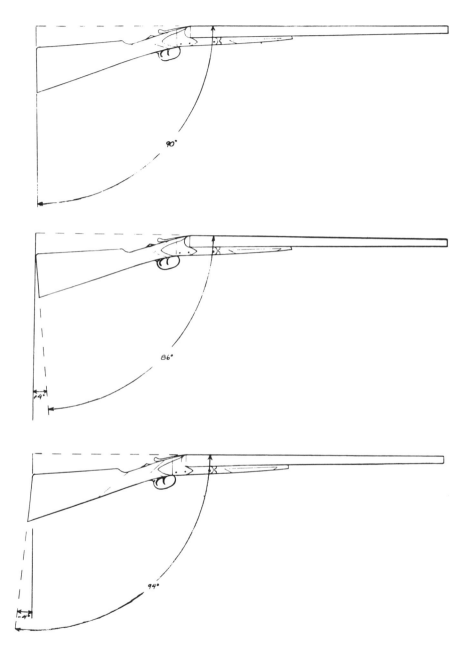

Pitch is the angle the butt of the stock forms with the barrels.

quire more pitch than a slim person. Women, obviously, are prime candidates for pitch. The bustier the woman the more pitch will be needed. Most men will find that 3 to 4 degrees of pitch will suit them quite well. Women usually require 6 or 7 degrees to make the stock most comfortable. An unfortunate situation that seems to occur rather frequently is a stock that has been shortened with no consideration given to pitch. The scenario usually goes something like this: a well-intentioned husband is trying to interest his wife in wing shooting. He knows enough about gun fit to realize that his wife, who is 6 inches shorter than he is, will not be comfortable with one of his guns. She obviously needs a shorter length of pull. He makes the supreme sacrifice and cuts down the stock of one of his guns. His intentions are good but his knowledge of gun fit is lacking. He sets the miter gauge on his table saw at 90 degrees and while blinking back the tears cuts an inch off the butt stock. The gun is now much easier for his wife to shoulder and he feels like a real hero. The problem arises when he takes her out to shoot. After only a few shots she complains that the toe of the stock is digging into her chest, and she does not want to shoot anymore. The male chauvinism in him wells up and he kicks himself for having cut the stock in the first place. If he had only been aware of pitch and cut the stock at an angle of 6 or 7 degrees from vertical his wife probably would not have been bothered by the recoil.

The shape of the butt stock can also affect how the recoil is distributed. Some stocks are designed with a slight concavity at the butt. This gives the stock a graceful appearance but it can be uncomfortable to shoot. The problem is that the toe of the stock becomes slightly pointed and some shooters find that this digs into their chest. Women in particular are bothered by this style of stock. A stock with a straight butt and slightly rounded toe is generally preferred by women.

Pitch will also affect how high a gun will shoot. Increasing pitch makes a gun shoot lower; decreasing pitch makes it shoot higher. This is most easily visualized if we think of anchoring the stock firmly on the shoulder and then increasing or decreasing pitch. As we change pitch we are changing the angle of the barrels relative to the butt. If the pitch is increased and the butt held firm on the shoulder the barrels will be angled down. Obviously, as pitch is decreased in this situation the barrels will be pointed higher. Some trap guns are designed with very little pitch or even with negative pitch. The techniques used for trap shooting are specialized and some shooters feel this style of stock gives them an advantage. Field gunners will usually find that a stock with between 3 and 7 degrees of pitch will suit them better.

Pitch can be measured in degree of angle with the aid of a protractor or a special gun-stock measuring tool. Many stock makers measure

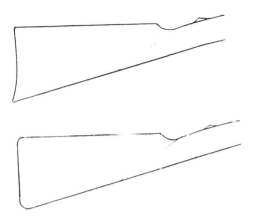

A slightly concave butt lends a graceful line to a stock, but can be uncomfortable for some shooters. A stock with a rounded toe is usually more comfortable, particularly for women shooters.

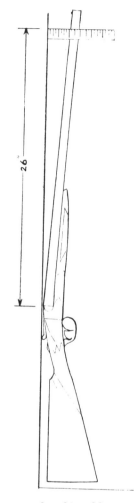

Measuring pitch in inches rather than degrees can be achieved by standing the gun on its butt and measuring the distance the barrels stand away from a vertical surface.

pitch by another technique. They stand the gun on its butt and push the receiver up against a plumbed vertical such as a door jamb or a wall. By measuring the distance between the barrels and the vertical one can determine pitch. It is critical that this measurement be taken at a standard distance from the breech. Obviously if we take this measurement at the muzzle of a gun with 32-inch barrels we will get a larger measurement than we would if we take the measurement on a gun with 26-inch barrels even though the stocks were identical. In order to equate this system to degrees, measure the distance the barrels stand away from the wall 26 inches from where the receiver touches the vertical surface. Using this system, ½-inch equals 1 degree of pitch. For example, most field guns are made with 4 degrees of pitch. If this gun were stood on its butt and pushed up against a wall the muzzle would be 2 inches away from the wall, presuming 26-inch barrels.

Aside from the measurements thus far discussed, there are several other aspects of a stock that can affect how it suits a shooter. The butt plate or recoil pad can affect how easily the gun comes to shoulder. Hard plastic or metal butt plates are strong and will not catch on clothing as the gun is raised to shoulder. The same holds true for a checkered wood butt. They do not offer any relief from recoil, however. If you are not particularly recoil-sensitive a hard butt plate or checkered wood butt will be most practical, particularly if your hunting does not involve a great deal of shooting. Most upland hunters just don't have the opportunity to fire a great number of shots in the course of a day. They are restrained by their hunting situation. The loads used are typically light and recoil is not a major consideration.

Anyone shooting heavy loads or doing a lot of shooting will find a recoil pad helpful. A typical day in the field may involve no more than a dozen shots, but what about the day you decide to sharpen your eye on clay targets? A well-designed recoil pad can make most any gun

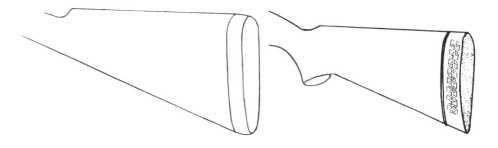

A smooth rubber- or leather-covered recoil pad is less likely to catch on clothing as the gun is mounted. The ventilated, pebble-finish rubber pads have a tendency to cling to clothing as the gun is shouldered.

more pleasant to shoot. When choosing a recoil pad for a field gun you
have to be careful. A pad that works well on a skeet or trap gun or on
your rifle may be a hindrance on a field gun. Many of the recoil pads
produced today are designed for competitive-style shooters, i.e. trap
and skeet shooters, or for rifle shooters. These individuals want a pad
that will soften the blow and will stay put. Trap and skeet in this
country is most often shot with a preshouldered gun. Once the gun is
positioned on the shoulder and cheek the skeet and trap enthusiast
does not want it to slide about on the shoulder. A rifle shooter has a
similar need—once his rifle is in position he does not want it to slide.
Ventilated rubber recoil pads with a pebble-like finish fulfil the needs
of most competitive and rifle shooters. This style of recoil pad is not
ideal for a field shooter, however, because it tends to catch on clothing
as the gun is brought to shoulder. The field gunner must mount his
gun in one smooth motion; there is generally no time to fidget. A recoil
pad that clings to your jacket or vest can be a real nuisance. So a field
gun should have a smooth pad that will slip over clothing easily. The
solid rubber pads with a smooth surface are better suited to a field
gun. Perhaps the best of all are the leather-covered recoil pads. They
are very smooth and will not cling to your clothing as you mount the
gun to shoulder. The leather-covered pad has just one drawback: it's
expensive. If you can stand the price, such a pad is a nice addition to
any field gun.

*Pistol grips work well with a single trigger but can make double triggers more difficult
to use.*

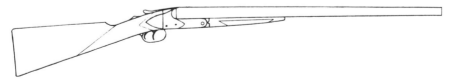

*A straight grip is preferred with double triggers and is perfectly suitable for a single
trigger as well.*

Another aspect of stock design that should be considered is pistol grip verses straight grip. If the gun has a single trigger, I don't believe there is any significant difference in function. Choose whatever style stock feels most comfortable to your hand. If the gun has double triggers then I feel a straight grip is advisable. To best operate double triggers, the trigger hand should be free to move ever so slightly. A pistol grip makes double triggers more difficult to use because it restricts the mobility of the trigger hand. With a straight grip it is much easier to shuffle the trigger hand back to operate the rear trigger.

Some people theorize that the straight grip creates a more natural alignment between the hands. The hands seem to work together most naturally when they are held in the same plane, and the straight grip keeps the trigger hand closer to the line of the lead hand. I would not argue with the theory. I like straight grips, but have worked with many people who did not. Choose the grip shape that seems to fit your hand best.

5

The Master
Eye

Should you shoot with both eyes open or one eye closed? Most people are best advised to shoot with both eyes open. Assuming your eye and hand dominance is on the same side you will generally find that shooting with both eyes open will give you the best advantage. With both eyes open your peripheral vision and depth perception are enhanced. If you are cross-dominant, then there may be very good reason to close one eye as you shoot. The determining factor is whether your strong hand and your strong eye are on the same side. Everyone is aware of hand dominance, but many people are unaware that they also have a dominant eye. In most cases eye and hand dominance will be on the same side; that is, if your right hand is your strong hand your right will be the dominant or master eye.

When pointing at an object the alignment is made with only one eye, the master eye. Because of the distance between the eyes, it is impossible to use both. The finger, or shotgun barrel, or whatever we are pointing with, will be pulled into alignment between the stronger of our eyes and the object we are looking at. We do not control which eye will dominate. Eye dominance, like hand dominance, is something you are born with. What is important in wing shooting is that your eye and hand dominance be uniform. It does not matter one whit whether you are right- or left-dominant. What is important is that if you are right-handed that you are also right-eyed; most people are.

How do you determine which eye is your master eye? Easy—simply point at something with both eyes open. Presuming you are right-handed, close your left eye. If you still appear to be pointing at the object, you are right-eye dominant. To give yourself a better appreciation of the phenomenon, try the test again. This time after you have

When pointing at an object the alignment is made with only one eye, the master eye. As long as we are not holding a gun the issue of cross dominance is of little importance.

pointed at an object with both eyes open, close your right eye. You will find that with only the left eye open your finger will be pointed several inches to the right of the object you originally focused on. (I am presuming that you are like most people, and you have a dominant right hand and eye.)

If you are left-handed use the same test, but after having made your initial point with both eyes open, close your right eye. Presumably you will find that with just the left eye open you are still on target. Most people will find that their eye and hand dominance is uniform. What if you do not? What if you are a right-hander and find that after pointing at an object with both eyes open and then closing the left eye you are no longer lined up? First, try the test again. Don't jump to any hasty conclusions. You may find it easier to determine eye dominance if you use a piece of paper with a hole in it. Cut a hole about the size of a nickel in the middle of a sheet of paper. Hold the paper out at arm's length and use the hole in the paper like a peep sight. Pick a small object ten to twenty feet away and center the object in the hole in the paper. Now close your left eye. If the object remains centered in the hole you are right eye dominant. If the object disappears from view you are left eye dominant. If you do determine that your eye and hand dominance are not the same, don't despair. You can still become a great wing shot!

If you are cross-dominant you should not shoot from the shoulder of your strong hand and keep both eyes open. If you do, you will be frustrated. Your natural pointing reflex will not align your gun with your line of sight. The gun will align naturally with the line of sight only when the shooting shoulder is on the same side as the dominant eye. When the shooting shoulder and dominant eye are on opposite

The shooter on the left is right-handed and right-eyed and is pointing his gun in the direction he is looking. The shooter on the right is cross-dominant, right-handed and left-eyed. He will shoot across his line of vision and consistently shoot left.

sides the gun will be canted across the line of sight. A cross-dominant shooter has three options. He can learn to shoot from the shoulder of the weak hand. He can close the dominant eye as the gun is brought to shoulder. Lastly, he can use a cross-over stock. Let's consider each option.

If the shooter can manage it, learning to shoot from the shoulder of the weak hand is probably the best course. Shooting will come more naturally if the gun is on the side of the dominant eye. If the individual is young and new to shooting I would encourage him to try switching shoulders. You find some people who make the conversion quite easily. It's not uncommon to discover people who were probably naturally left-handed and have been forced to become righties. To my knowledge it is impossible to force a change in eye dominance. Your parents, teachers, or drill sargent may have been able to cajole or beat you into a right-handed mold, but the eye is not affected. In such a case the person is not truly cross-dominant. You also find some people who are left-handed in all activities except shooting. They had been forced to shoot right-handed in the military and continued to shoot right-handed when they picked up a shotgun. In any of these cases, moving the gun to the opposite shoulder is usually an easy change.

But what if the individual does not find the transition easy? Some people are truly cross-dominant and find the shoulder switch difficult. They are strongly right-handed and equally strongly left-eyed, or vice versa. I usually suggest such people try closing their dominant eye as the gun comes to shoulder. If they can learn to do this, it is an expedient solution to the problem of cross dominance. The shooter can use both eyes until the last instant. He can take advantage of peripheral vision and depth perception to locate the bird and judge its range. Only after the decision to shoot has been made and the gun starts toward the shoulder is the eye closed. Very little is sacrificed with this technique. Many shooters find that closing the dominant eye just prior to shooting is a workable solution to cross dominance. But there are some people who find it nearly impossible to close the dominant eye without closing both eyes. They cannot wink their strong eye.

Such shooters might try wearing glasses with a piece of tape near the top of the lens on the side of the dominant eye. Obscuring the vision of the master eye in such a fashion could be tried by any cross-dominant shooter. I wouldn't resort to this technique unless I had exhausted the above-mentioned solutions first. The problem with taping over the lens of glasses is deciding how much to obscure. If you totally block the vision of one eye you lose depth perception and peripheral vision. Many people feel very uncomfortable, like they are about to step over a bank, or into a hole, if the vision of one eye is blocked. Obviously if you don't

A small piece of tape on the top portion of the lens of shooting glasses can sometimes help a cross-dominant shooter.

block the master eye enough it may continue to dominate and cause all the misalignment problems. There is a happy middle ground, and I have seen some cross-dominant shooters who responded beautifully to a piece of tape on their glasses. It was small enough to have minimal effect on depth perception and peripheral vision, yet large enough to force the weak eye to make the alignment. If you decide to try using tape, put it close to the top of the lens. This will usually eliminate the feeling of vertigo because you can still see down. It will not have a marked effect on your vision until you try to look through the top of the lenses, as you do when in shooting position. Experiment with the size and location of the tape on the lens. You might try using a transparent tape, like Scotch tape. I have seen some shooters who found that a small piece of Scotch tape was enough to force the weak eye into making the alignment. The slight blurring created by the Scotch tape was hardly noticed until the head was in shooting position.

The last resort is a cross-over stock. This style of stock has a severe bend or cast. The stock is bent to the degree that the barrels are brought into alignment with the eye opposite from the shoulder to which the gun is mounted. I consider this a last resort because of the difficulty in fitting this style of stock. I have never seen a try gun that had sufficient range of adjustment to be used for fitting cross-over stocks, though they may well exist. Most experienced gun fitters can arrive at a reasonably accurate set of stock dimensions by watching someone shoot, and perhaps having them mount two or three guns of different dimensions. This is educated guesswork and is never as reliable as working with a try gun. Attempting this kind of guesswork with a cross-over stock is extremely tricky. If a gun fitter had two or three cross-over stocks for a shooter to try, the process would be made much easier, but seldom is this the case. It is just not feasible for most gun makers to keep trial cross-over guns at the ready for the rare individual who needs one. To compound the problem, you would need stocks that were bent both left and right if you were to accomodate everyone. Attempting to fit a shooter with a cross-over stock is most difficult. The London gun makers probably have more experience in the design of this style of stock than anyone. If you determine that there is no other solution to your problem of cross dominance, be sure that your gun fitter is confident and experienced with the cross-over design.

Fortunately, the shooter who requires a cross-over stock is rare. Most cross-dominant individuals can find an easier solution. The simplest is learning to close one eye as the gun is raised to shoulder. Best of all, most people need not concern themselves with cross dominance, because their eye and hand dominance is uniform. They can keep both eyes open and give it their best shot.

A subject I hesitate to broach, because of a lack of scientific support (and a real fear of making offense when none is intended), is women's propensity to use the wrong eye when shooting. I am not sure whether women truly have a tendency to be cross-dominant or whether their predilection to align with the eye opposite from that to which their gun is shouldered is due to unfamiliarity with guns. Whatever the case may be, I have found that many women shooters have greater success if they close the eye opposite the shooting shoulder.

I believe that what I have observed with regard to women using the wrong eye is related to their lack of experience with guns. I would guess that fifty percent of the ladies I have worked with had little or no shooting experience. Perhaps ten percent of the male students I have coached could be similarly classified. It is my belief that if an individual is not familiar with looking over the barrel of a gun, the presence of the barrel in the field of vision can be confusing. I believe that the vision of the eye on the side of the shooting shoulder is sufficiently obscured to force the new shooter to align with their off eye (the eye opposite the shooting shoulder). The weaker eye will take over if the vision of the master eye is obscured. New shooters sometimes align with the weak eye because they have mounted the gun clumsily and block the vision of the strong eye. This is usually a temporary phenomenon. As the gun-mounting technique polishes and the shooter becomes more accustomed to looking over the gun barrel, the problem usually disappears.

6

Lead And The Psychology of Wing Shooting

No one would argue the necessity for leading a moving target, but there is differing opinion on how best to judge the amount. If you are shooting in a controlled situation like skeet, actually calculating the amount of lead necessary for each shot makes great sense. Attempting to calculate leads in the game field is mighty tough sledding. The field shooter needs a system that does not require conscious calculations based on a knowledge of the bird's speed, range, and angle of flight. He needs an instinctive system that will capitalize on his eye's ability to determine lead.

The English method is just such a system. It relies on the eye's instinctive capabilities and a gun-mounting style that will incorporate lead into the swing without conscious thought. The gun-mounting technique is designed to create sufficient momentum in the gun and the shooter to carry the muzzles through the target and automatically establish the correct lead. It does not require the shooter to be conscious of the exact amount he is leading the bird.

The theory is that the speed of the target will determine the amount of momentum in the swing. A fast-moving target will require the shooter to swing his body and gun rapidly and thereby develop sufficient momentum to carry his gun well beyond the target as the shooter fires. A slow-moving bird requires less speed and therefore less momentum. The gun will swing through the target only a modest amount. The theory works extremely well at the short to medium ranges typical of most upland hunting situations.

61

Lead is a by-product of a good swing, just as hitting a golf ball straight down the middle of the fairway is a by-product of a good swing. Everything from the stance on up contributes to the overall success. Lead cannot be discussed out of context; it is a part of the whole. Unfortunately, most shooters consider lead a topic separate from gun mounting, stance, hand placement, or any of the other aspects of good shooting technique. Lead is *not* something that you add on just before pulling the trigger. Just the opposite is true for the field gunner. The lead should be a natural outflow of a properly executed swing.

In this country there are several accepted techniques for establishing lead, none of which is identical to the English system. Many shooters use what is termed a sustained lead system. They get the gun barrel a predetermined amount out in front of the bird and try to maintain this carefully measured amount as they shoot. If the situation is a controlled one like skeet, where speed, angle, and range are known, this can be a very effective way to shoot. Obviously the system is not well suited to most field shooting situations, with the possible exceptions of some types of pass shooting. If the shooter can see his target from sufficient distance to give him time to judge range and speed he might have a chance to calculate the right lead. If a gunner shoots from the same blind or in the same area for a number of years, he might log enough experience to give him a good feeling for leads necessary for particular shots. But in general the sustained lead technique is not an easy one to apply to the field. Upland, or walk-up shooting, doesn't lend itself to the sustained lead technique because things happen too quickly. I have never heard anyone suggest a sustained lead system for walk-up shooting—it is usually suggested for the pass shooter.

Snap, or spot, shooting is the term usually applied to the technique favored by the upland specialists. Rather than swinging the gun along a predetermined distance out in front of the target, the spot shooter pokes his gun to a spot out in front of the bird. This style of shooting is considered better suited to most upland game situations because it is quicker than a sustained-lead technique. I have seen a number of very fine spot shooters. The technique does work, but it is not nearly as easy as it might seem. Good spot shooters are usually those lucky few who have great natural eye–hand coordination and timing.

The difficulty with spot shooting is that the gun stops at the instant of fire. Good spot shooters usually have fast reflexes. They are able to snap the gun to shoulder and fire immediately. Without lightning reflexes, you tend to shoot well behind the target. If your timing falters the least little bit the bird will fly past your gun in a split second. If your gun is moving with the target, as with the sustained-lead system, timing is much less critical.

Let's consider a bird crossing at a 90-degree angle, thirty yards from the shooter and traveling thirty mph. A charge of shot is traveling 1200 feet per second when it exits the muzzle. Without taking into account the deceleration of the shot over thirty yards, it would take the shot 0.075 seconds to cover the distance. During the .075 seconds the bird would travel 3.3 feet. Obviously this is the amount of lead we need. Providing you were able to ascertain speed, angle, and range and make the calculation for lead, you would still need near-perfect timing to make the spot shooting technique work. If you err by as little as a few hundredths of a second you will miss. A sustained lead shooter, however, has margin for error in his timing, because the muzzle is presumably traveling along about three and a half feet out in front of the bird.

The obvious problem with both spot shooting and the sustained lead technique is the necessity for calculating the lead, either consciously or (in the case of the best spot shooters) by instinct, aided by much practice. Spot shooters especially must have great reflexes.

Unfortunately most people are predisposed to spot shoot. It appears to be an easy and logical way to down a bird that is crossing or incoming. It would seem that the shooter would gain an advantage, or head start, if he pointed his gun in the path of the oncoming bird and picked him off as he flew in front of the waiting gun—it's the old "ambush 'em at the pass" theory. But what may look good on paper does not always hold up in practice. This is a case in point. If the gun is stationary and the target is moving you have created a shooting situation that requires split-second timing; timing too demanding for most people.

The system closest to the English technique is usually referred to as "swing-through" in this country. The shooter mounts his gun to shoulder and initially points it behind his target. He then sweeps the muzzle past the target and fires as the gun is pulling away in front. There are various forms of the swing-through technique. Some shooters fire as soon as they see daylight between the barrel and the bird. Others hold fire until they are a predetermined distance out in front. Obviously, this latter variation comes very close to a sustained lead system. It requires shooters to be conscious of the amount of lead they are using.

In its purest form the swing-through practitioner is not conscious of how much he is leading. He sweeps the gun past the target and as soon as he is in front he fires. This is very much like the English system in that it relies on gun momentum to establish the proper lead. The English technique is a refinement of the swing-through system. Perhaps it would be more accurate to say the swing-through system as preached in this country is a bastardization of the English technique.

How do the two systems differ, and why is the English system better suited to most field-shooting situations? The styles differ principally with regard to when the swing-through takes place. The target is passed subsequent to the gun mount in the American version. The English style requires the shooter to pass the target during the gun mount. It may seem as though I am splitting hairs, but the difference is a most significant one. The American swing-through shooter brings his gun fully to shoulder and cheek and intentionally points the muzzles behind the bird. The next step is a swing that will carry the gun beyond the bird as he fires. This style does not take best advantage of natural pointing abilities. He has used that natural pointing gesture to direct the gun to the wrong spot—behind the bird. Secondly, the shooter must now make his swing with the barrels in the middle of his field of vision.

Wouldn't it be easier to start the swing as the gun was coming up to the shoulder? Start the lateral motion, or swing, at the beginning and build it into the gun mount, rather than trying to add it at the end. When a bird flushes, or swings over the decoys, our first response should not be to snap the gun to cheek and shoulder, as is so frequently the case. We must train ourselves to start the gun moving along with the target and keep the body square to the direction of fire. In this way the gun mount and swing are integrated. The shooter keeps his eye riveted on the bird and pushes his lead hand (left hand for a right-handed shooter) at his target as though he were pointing it out. You actually have the impression that you are shooting almost directly at the target, but in fact the momentum of your swing carries you beyond your target as the gun is fired. With this style of gun mounting you take best advantage of your instinctive pointing abilities and decrease the likelihood of being visually distracted by the gun. The gun is not in the middle of the field of vision until the last instant. This is the moment the shot should be taken.

If you can learn to steel yourself, and supress the reflex to snap the gun fully to shoulder as a preliminary to any other motion, you will be well on the way to developing a swing that will carry you through the target. The key is learning to swing *through* rather than *to* the target. You are trying to develop a style that will build lead naturally into the swing; a system that will naturally lead the bird and not require you to consciously calculate lead and add it at the end.

I have heard the English technique described as one which does not require lead. This is of course incorrect. The only way to decrease the necessity for lead is to increase the speed of the shot charge. The English technique can only make the lead seem more natural. In practice, we are not conscious that we are leading the bird. We may actually be left with the impression that we shot directly at the bird because

Many shooters mount the gun to shoulder before there is any lateral motion, or swing. This shooter has completed the gun mount too early.

The swing and the mount must be integrated. We must train ourselves to start the gun and body moving along with the target as we mount the gun to shoulder. The gun should not meet the cheek until the last instant when the shot is taken.

No matter what the angle, we must supress the reflex to snap the gun to shoulder as a preliminary to any other motion. The gun must come to shoulder smoothly and meet the cheek only at the very last instant when then the shot is taken.

our visual attention remains focused there. We must be careful not to be misled. The field gunner must push his lead hand and gun muzzle *through* the target, not just *to* it.

The inexperienced shooter has a natural tendency to tighten his muscles and look down at the barrels at the instant of fire. This will inevitably cause your gun to stop and you will shoot behind your bird almost every time. You must train yourself to keep your eye on the bird and flow through the target with a relaxed, smooth swing. Students of tennis or golf have a similar problem. They look up at the critical instant when they are about to make contact with the ball, and they tighten up as they strike the ball. Relax and follow through is advice that could be given to students of any eye–hand activity.

As the range increases, it is particularly important for English-style shooters to keep in mind that they are not shooting directly at the target. They may be left with that impression because of their visual concentration on the target, but the momentum of the swing is in fact carrying them beyond the bird at the instant of fire. You must allow your gun to flow through and beyond the bird as you fire. The trick, if we may call it that, is to be sure you let your gun drift out in front but to *ignore exactly how far in front you are*. This may sound like strange advice, but it is at the heart of an accomplished field shooter's technique. As the range increases, he becomes increasingly aware that his gun has passed the bird as he fires, but he cannot tell you exactly how much he leads each bird. If you try to engineer things too precisely, you will lose.

If a shooter becomes overly conscious of the gap between his barrel and the bird, he will usually stop his swing. Visual concentration must remain on the bird. Upland shooting seldom allows time for us to become overly conscious of anything. Pass shooting generally allows more time for us to confuse ourselves. The bird that can be seen from a long distance is often the most difficult target. We raise our guns prematurely and try to measure things too precisely. In our attempt to align everything to the last millimeter, we break visual concentration on the bird, focus on the gap between the barrel and the bird and stop our swing. As we pull the trigger, we may feel like this one is as good as in the bag—and we generally shoot four feet behind it.

Lead is present in every situation, whether you are shooting bobwhites in heavy cover or pass shooting geese. At close to moderate range it comes so naturally that we may think it has vanished entirely. It hasn't. If your swing is made properly and you keep your eye on the bird the lead is built in. What we must be mindful of is not to take it out. All too frequently I have peered over the shoulder of a student and watched as he executed a shot perfectly until the last split second. The technique was good and the lead was perfect, but at the last instant he breaks confidence and tenses up. His gun stops and he misses. At that last, critical moment, he looks down at his gun, or tries to see exactly how far out in front he is. This will inevitably stop the swing.

Confidence is an important ingredient in all eye–hand activities, and wing shooting is no exception. Mental attitude is particularly important in pass-shooting situations where there is time to think. Have you ever noticed that the unexpected shot is the one you often make? A bird flushes when you least expect it, and without any thought your gun comes to shoulder and the shot is fired. Your hunting companion is duly impressed by your technique, and you modestly say "guess I got lucky on that one." It wasn't luck, it was the fact that the bird caught you by surprise and totally captured your visual attention. Your eye and hand worked together, unimpeded by the wheels between your ears.

One of the keys to becoming an accomplished pass shooter is the ability to remain relaxed and confident as you watch the bird approach. This is easier said than done, but crucial to success. If you can channel your energies visually you will improve your score. Make yourself look at just one part of the bird. Don't look at the whole; make yourself look only at his eye or his bill. It is really of little consequence what part of the bird you focus on, but I would suggest something on the eating end. It seems more beneficial to look at the head, rather than the tail. If you look at a part rather than the whole you will be less likely to break visual concentration. Like the golfer staring at just one dimple on his ball, the wing shooter can gain an edge in concentration. If we can maintain this high degree of visual concentration it seems to occupy the mind and prevent you from overthinking the shot.

Be able to accept a miss. No one in the history of wing shooting has ever gone straight. Mulling over a miss will only destroy your timing. Often I have had a student turn to me in disgust and say "What happened? I know I was on that one." He is usually correct, but not in the manner he meant. Yes he was right on the target. He had taken a little extra time and really aimed the shot. His gun had slowed as he tried to be doubly sure and as he pulled the trigger the bird was lined up right off the end of a stationary gun. He took the lead out of a good swing because his timing was slow. His timing was slow because he lacked confidence. He lacked confidence because he was fretting over a previous miss.

Don't become overly diagnostic while you are in the field. If you try to figure out where you missed each bird, you will be in for a long day of figuring. The student who wants to know where he missed every shot is missing the point. He is still thinking in terms of aiming. The way to hit the next bird is not by compensating for a mistake you made on the last. Even if you are consistently shooting high, or low, or where-ever it may be, the way to correct is not by consciously aiming to the opposite side. The way to correct your problem is to find the flaw in style, or in the fit of your gun. If you are consistently shooting high, perhaps you have too much weight on your back foot, or perhaps your lead hand is too far forward. You may not be cheeking the gun firmly enough, or the gun may not have sufficient drop to suit you. Find out *why*, not *where*—there is an enormous difference.

7

Safety And Shooting Etiquette

Teaching people how to hit what they are shooting at is what this book is all about, but there is a much more important issue germaine to every shooting situation: how to prevent shooting something you don't want to. Before anyone attempts to learn how to shoot they *must* have thorough knowledge of gun safety. Firearms are dangerous in the same way automobiles are dangerous. If they are used properly and good judgment and common sense prevail there is no reason to fear them. If they are put in the wrong hands and used carelessly there is a potential for harm. All in all, I feel a lot safer when I am in the field hunting than when I am on a crowded freeway.

Hunter safety courses are mandatory in many states. As my grandfather was so fond of saying, "So mote it be," and a hearty amen. No one should pick up a firearm until they have a thorough understanding of its safe operation. First, hands-on instruction is required. I would not want any new shooter to read a few pages in this book or any other and feel he was ready to load and fire.

The basic rules of gun safety are simple. Do not point a gun at anything you don't intend shooting and always treat a gun as though it were loaded. Gun safety is common sense and courtesy. When not actively hunting or on the firing line at the practice range keep the action of your gun open and of course empty. Don't be in too great a hurry to load your gun whether afield or at the practice range. The individual who is stuffing shells in the gun before the car door has closed will never get another shooting invitation from me.

In my experience, most people are very conscious of the basic rules of gun safety. Rare indeed is the shooter who truly doesn't know. Careless is the operative word. Of the hundreds of shooters I have dealt with only a handful were truly careless, but it takes only one. Never be reticent about reminding a shooter if he becomes careless. This is no time for diplomacy; be polite, but be direct.

A number of years ago I witnessed a shooter being justifiably rebuked for taking dangerously low shots. It was on a driven shoot in Europe and one individual was shooting too close to the line of beaters. The game keeper of the estate on which we were shooting pointed this out to the shooter, who was of course very embarrassed. I don't believe the fellow in question was as reckless as he was excitable. This was a new experience and he wanted to put in a good performance. The lesson is this: never be embarrassed to hold your fire. There is no bird in the world worth taking a risky shot for. If for any reason you don't feel totally comfortable and in control, don't shoot. This is particularly important in new situations. Ease into it.

Another side of gun safety is the proper care and feeding of the gun to insure that it does not malfunction and injure the shooter. The most common accident in this vein for the shotgunner is an obstruction in the barrel. It takes only a little bit of mud or snow to plug up a shotgun barrel with disastrous consequences. I make it a habit to check the barrel before loading. I prefer breaking guns to magazine-style guns for several reasons, and among them is the ease of detecting any foreign object in the barrels when loading.

Not only must we be careful to prevent the muzzle from becoming obstructed, but we must be mindful of what goes in from the breech end as well. A roll of lifesavers, Tums, or a tube of lipstick all feel rather like a shotgun shell if they are fished out of a pocket hurriedly. If the shooting is fast, as in a dove field, or on a driven shoot or tower shoot, the gun may be loaded more by feel than by sight. The Tums fall through the chamber and lodge in the barrel. The shooter raises his gun and pulls the trigger. Nothing happens. Thinking he dropped the shell on the previous loading attempt, the shooter reaches hurriedly into his pocket and loads without checking the barrels. When he pulls the trigger this time there is real trouble. This may sound far-fetched, but it has happened. Don't let it happen to you.

Never mix ammunition of any type in your pocket. The Tums scenario could just as likely, or perhaps even more likely, have involved a smaller-gauge shell. A twenty-gauge shotgun shell will fall through the chamber of a twelve-gauge gun and lodge in the barrel. A twelve-gauge shell may then be loaded and the gun will fire. I don't believe it is necessary to go into gory detail about the consequences. A twenty-eight-gauge shell will have the same effect on a sixteen-gauge gun. Carry only the shells appropriate to the gun you have in your hands.

Never fire a gun with ammunition longer than the chamber. Shotguns are made with different chamber lengths. Most shotgun ammunition manufactured today is designed for use in guns with chambers 2¾ inches or longer. Most modern shotguns have either 2¾- or 3-inch chambers, but over the years many guns were produced with shorter chambers. Chambers as short as two inches have been used in some European guns, and 2½- and 2⁹/₁₆-inch chambers are not rare. You can't determine whether a shell is appropriate for the chamber by measuring an unfired shell and relating that to the chamber length of your gun. It is the length of the shell *after* being fired, when the crimp has opened, that is important. First, know what the chamber length of your gun is. If it is not marked plainly on the barrel or action, take your gun to a knowledgeable gunsmith, or dealer, and let him determine the length. If your gun has a 2¾-inch chamber you may shoot that length or any shorter shell, but never fire 3-inch ammo in the gun. Only use 3-inch if your gun has 3-inch chambers. If you own an older gun with 2-, 2½- or 2⁹/₁₆-inch chambers do not use 2¾-inch ammunition. It is unlikely the gun will explode if you use ammunition only slightly longer than the chamber, (i.e. 2¾-inch ammo in a 2½- or 2⁹/₁₆-inch chambered gun) but the pressure developed in the chamber will undoubtedly be higher than it was designed to tolerate. The gun will be over-stressed when fired with ammunition that is too long. You will damage the gun and run the risk of injury to yourself and the gun if you persist in using the wrong length shell.

If you purchase a used gun, be sure it is in sound working order before firing it. Be sure the gun has modern fluid steel barrels, as opposed to damascus steel, if you are using modern ammunition. Be sure the gun was proof tested for the ammunition you intend using. If this all sounds confusing to you, have a good gunsmith inspect any used gun you are considering buying before you hand over the money.

There is one more precaution I would strongly suggest. Do not fire any gun unless you are wearing some type of protective glasses. If an accident should occur, your eyes are most vulnerable. The best pair of shooting glasses you can buy is mighty cheap insurance. Along the same lines, I would suggest using some type of hearing protectors if you are going to do any volume of shooting. This is not accident insurance, but a means of protection yourself from the tiny bit of damage that is done every time you are subjected to a very loud noise. You will slowly lose your hearing if you don't shield your ears in some manner. Either ear plugs or the ear muff protector should be used. This is particularly important at practice sessions where you are likely to do more shooting than in the field, and you will probably be close by other shooters.

I have to admit that I do not use any hearing protection when upland shooting. Our New England grouse and woodcock shooting seldom heats up the barrels with action. Even if more shooting were involved, I doubt I would wear any type of protection. The reason is that hearing is important to the game. You have to be able to hear the bell on your dog, or better yet hear when it stops. You often hear a bird flush before you see it, if you see it at all. Hearing is essential to the experience, so we sacrifice a little bit of the sense we so depend on every time we go afield. If hearing is not essential to the game, as in practice sessions, or tower shoots, and there is likely to be a lot of shooting, protect your ears.

I want to reemphasize the need for learning safe gun handling procedures first hand. Don't go to the practice range or afield until you have had the benefit of personal instruction from a qualified individual.

8

Tools

Most people are familiar with the Currier and Ives print depicting a barefoot boy with cane pole, worms and full stringer, in counterpoint to the well dressed and well equipped angler fruitlessly plying the stream. A quaint bit of Americana, but have you ever known a bent-pin fisherman who, by virtue of his pin, was more successful than the will equipped angler? Stories about barefoot kids out-fishing and out-shooting their well equipped adult counterparts seem to be part of the lore and legend of American field sports. Understandably no one wants to play the role of the over-equipped, hapless dandy. We would all prefer to think of ourselves as the barefoot kid who by virtue of native skill can out-shoot, out-fish and out-anything the well equipped slicker attempts.

Why is it that this barefoot boy syndrome seems so common among shooters? I have known individuals who seem to pride themselves on the shabbiness of their hunting clothes. These people would not consider mowing their lawn, much less going to the golf course, similarly clad. Some shooters exhibit a similar attitude toward their guns. They seem to feel that an inexpensive, beat up old gun is a badge of honor. If you're of the barefoot-boy school, ask yourself what the kid, who blew their socks off with an old ill-fitting gun, could have done if he had good equipment?

Good equipment is nothing to be embarrassed about. A fine gun will not make a poor shooter great overnight, but it can help. An ill-fit, ill-balanced gun will handicap anyone. I can find no virtue in choosing to dress shabbily and shoot an old clunker. Most people can't afford a best grade London side lock, but buy the best you can. You don't have to spend thousands to insure a good quality gun. The single most impor-

73

tant thing is not the price tag, but the fit (see Chapter 4). If you can afford a custom fit gun, great. If you can't, shop until you find a production gun that fits well or can be altered to fit.

The relative merits of various types of shotguns have been the topic of much discussion. Auto-loaders, pumps, over-unders, side-by-sides and any other configuration of shotgun you can name has its loyal supporters. I am not inclined to add my two cents to the melée. If an individual has confidence in a gun, or a particular type of action, that is usually worth more than all the theoretical arguments. There is no one gun that will suit every shooter's needs in every situation.

Although I don't intend to discuss the relative merits of the various designs, I would like to make one comparative observation. I am more comfortable when those around me are using breaking guns. I am not saying magazine-style actions are inherently more dangerous than breaking guns. My point is that auto-loaders and pumps make me more skittish. The reason is simple. The top lever on a breaking gun is easy to operate and once the gun is open I can relax a bit. When the action is open, it is obvious if the gun is loaded. Although it is easy to open the action of an auto-loader or a pump, there is still the question of whether there are shells in the magazine. It takes close scrutiny to determine if shells remain there. It also takes more time and effort to remove the shells from the magazine than to pluck them from the chambers of a side by side or over-under. It is easier to open and unload a breaking gun than a magazine gun, and for this reason more shooters seem inclined to do so.

There can be no argument that the shooter, not the gun, determines how safe any situation will be. A good gun handler will be safe no matter what he is shooting. A careless gun handler can't be made safe by the use of a particular type of gun.

Rather than debate the respective merits of various actions I would like to discuss an issue that is pertinent to every style shotgun, yet in my opinion has not received adequate recognition. Most shooters consider barrel length to be a function of the shooting situation. I contend that the length of barrels a shooter uses should be governed as much by his size and physique as by the type of shooting he will be doing.

The old theory has always been short barrels for upland shooting in heavy cover and long barrels for waterfowl. The notion that long barrels shoot farther or "harder" has been for the most part dispelled, as it well should be. Most people realize that with modern ammunition there is no ballistic necessity for barrels in excess of about two feet. Yet most hunters will persist in using long barrels for waterfowl shooting and short barrels in the uplands. Why this custom persists is variously explained by the necessity for short barrels in close quarters and the advantage of a longer sighting plane in the duck blind. I'm not convinced of the efficacy of these arguments. If one accepts the instinctive point theory and the necessity for total visual concentration on the target, the sighting plane theory loses weight. The theory that a short barrel is always preferable in heavy cover does not jibe with my experience.

The size and physique of the shooter should be what determines barrel length. The effect barrel length has on balance and overall weight is more important than how far apart the trees are or any sighting radius arguments. Every knowledgeable shooter will agree that good balance is important in a shotgun. What constitutes good balance is a question for debate. Every shooter has his own preference, but most people agree that the weight should be more or less evenly distributed between the hands. That is, the balance point of the gun should be approximately half-way between the points where the hands grip the gun. Some prefer a gun that is a little barrel-heavy, others like them barrel-light, but the differences are slight.

Once you decide what feels good to you, why change? Why change the weight and balance of your gun to conform to some old theory about longer barrels for the duck marsh? The hunter who switches from a 26- to a 30-inch barrel has obviously changed the balance of his gun. Unless something is done to the stock to counteract the additional barrel weight, the balance point has been moved forward. If this same individual is fortunate enough to own two guns, one for upland and the other for waterfowl shooting, he may also have opted for a slightly shorter stock on his waterfowl gun (see Chapter 3 on gun fit). As discussed earlier, the heavy clothes often needed during the waterfowl season add to length of pull. If a gun is to be used while wearing heavy clothes it makes sense to decrease the length of pull a bit. If we decrease the length of pull and increase barrel length we shift the balance point forward, and we wind up with a gun that is barrel-heavy.

If our two-gun hunter uses a shorter barrel and longer stock on his upland gun than on his waterfowl gun the feel of the two may become very different. If he uses a short-barrelled breaking gun with a long stock in the upland and a long-barrelled pump- or auto-loader with a short stock in the duck blind, he is dealing with radically different guns. Be careful that you don't move the balance point too far forward or back.

The barrel length should be related to the length and weight of the stock. If you are small and require a short stock, be wary of long barrels. If you are bigger than average and require a long stock be careful not to use too short a barrel. The extremes are all we need to avoid. Do not move the balance point of the gun too far from a spot halfway between your hands. On numerous occasions I have seen this rule violated. The two most common examples are auto-loaders with short stocks and long barrels and breaking guns with short barrels and long stocks.

The ill balanced auto-loader is usually created with the best intentions. A husband or father shortens the stock of a 30-inch full choke auto-loader to make it easier for a wife or child to shoot. Dad is an avid duck hunter and wants Mom or child to share his fun. He knows enough about gun fit to realize the necessity of shortening the stock, but he is a firm believer in the 30-inch barrel. The gun that he's created is extremely barrel-heavy. The young or female shooter trying to use this ill balanced beast typically does not have the arm strength that dear old Dad has and the combination is frustrating. If your length of pull is 13 inches you will probably not find 30-inch or 32-inch barrels comfortable, particularly on pumps or auto-loaders. Conversely if you use a 15-inch length of pull be wary of 25-inch barrels, particularly on breaking guns. I can remember more than one shooting student who in their attempt to create their "ultimate" upland gun found frustration. Typically a taller- and stronger-than-average shooter decides his ultimate quail gun would be a 5½-pound over-under or side-by-side with 25-inch barrels. They acquire such a gun and soon find that the standard 14-inch stock is much too short for them. They add a 1-inch rubber recoil pad to lengthen the stock. This creates a better length of pull, but moves the balance too far back. The gun is so muzzle-light that the shooter has great difficulty moving smoothly. They typically start and stop the gun very quickly. The barrels feel too light. Longer barrels are not always better in the duck blind any more than shorter barrels are always better for upland work. Keep things in balance as best you can. The length of barrel you use should be related to the length of the stock.

Discussions centering around best choking and shot size for various situations have been numerous. The topic is important, but like the question of which action is best, not within the bounds of this book. I would refer readers to *Shotgunning: The Art and the Science* by Bob Brister. Certainly many knowledgeable authors have dealt with the subject, but I find Brister's insights most interesting. My experience as an instructor has led me to believe that most shooters tend to use too much choke than too little. This is directly related to most folk's tendency to overestimate range. I occasionally ask students to estimate the distance they are shooting and they are generally on the long side.

This is particularly true when the targets are overhead. I had one student tell me that it would be nearly impossible to break a clay target at the range we were shooting with anything less than full choke. He was convince that his improved cylinder choking was not adequate. Fortunately there was another member of his group shooting an improved cylinder choke who broke about seventy percent of the targets.

The student who was convinced he needed a full choke was fortunate to be in a controlled situation where the effectiveness of the open choke could be graphically demonstrated. Had he been in a dove field or duck blind he no doubt would have clung to his theory and probably gone out and bought a new gun or new barrel with full choke. His next outing would have been even more frustrating than the last. His margin for error would be significantly less with the full choke and his likelihood of hitting anything decreased. This type of individual will many times try using larger shot on the theory that whatever they had previously been using was not capable of killing at this range. Don't allow yourself to fall into this trap. More choke and larger shot is seldom the solution for a wing shooter's ills.

Before you decide you need more choke, larger shot, or a new gun, determine if you are pointing your present gun in the right direction. This is easier said than done, but all too frequently we blame the tools when the technique is at fault. There is no virtue in electing to use an ill fit clumsy gun, but even the best of guns must be pointed in the right direction. Good technique and good tools complement one another. We need them both to reach our full potential. The game we hunt deserves nothing less from every one of us.

Index